TEACHER'S PET PUBLICATIONS

PUZZLE PACK
for
The View from Saturday

based on the book by
E. L. Konigsburg

Written by
Mary B. Collins

© 2006 Teacher's Pet Publications
All Rights Reserved

The materials in this packet are copyrighted
by Teacher's Pet Publications, Inc.

These pages may be duplicated by the purchaser
for use in the purchaser's own classroom.

Copying any of these materials and distributing them
for any other purpose is a violation of the copyright laws.

© 2006 Teacher's Pet Publications, Inc.
www.tpet.com

INTRODUCTION
If you already own the LitPlan for this title, this Puzzle Pack will refresh your Unit Resource Materials and Vocabulary Resource Materials sections plus give you additional materials you can substitute into the tests. If you do not already have a complete LitPlan, these pages will give you some supplemental materials to use with your own plan. There are two main groups of materials: one set for unit words (such as characters' names, symbols, places, etc.) and one set for vocabulary words associated with the book.

WORD LIST
There is a word list for both the unit words and the vocabulary words. These lists show you which words are being used in the materials and the clues or definitions being used for those words. You may want to give students a word list with clues/definitions to help them, or you may want students to only have a word list (without clues/definitions) if you want them to work a little harder. Both are available for duplication. The word lists can also be your "calling key" for the bingo games.

FILL IN THE BLANK AND MATCHING
There are 4 each of the fill in the blank and matching worksheets for both the unit and vocabulary words. These pages can be used either as extra worksheets for students or as objective parts of a unit test. They can be done individually if students need extra help or as a whole class activity to review the material covered.

MAGIC SQUARES
The magic squares not only reinforce the material covered but also work on reasoning and math skills. Many teachers have told us that their students really enjoy doing these!

WORD SEARCH PUZZLES
The word search words go in all directions, as indicated on your answer keys. Two of the word search puzzles have the clues listed rather than the words. This makes the puzzle a little more difficult, but it reinforces the material better. Two word search puzzles have words only for students who find the clue puzzles too difficult.

CROSSWORD PUZZLES
Both unit and vocabulary word sections have 4 crossword puzzles.

BINGO CARDS
There are 32 individual bingo cards for the unit words and 32 individual bingo cards for the vocabulary words. You can use your word list as a "call list," calling the words at random and marking them off of your list as you go, or you could use the flash cards by cutting them apart and drawing the words at random from a hat (or box or whatever). To make a better review, you might ask for the definition and spelling of each word as you call it out–or you could call out the definitions and have students tell you the words they need to look for on the puzzle.

JUGGLE LETTERS
The vocabulary juggle letter game is intended to help students learn the spellings of the words. One sheet has the definitions listed on it as an extra help for students who need it or to reinforce the definitions if you choose to do so.

FLASH CARDS
We've included a set of vocabulary flash cards you can duplicate, cut, and fold for your students. Some teachers make a few sets for general use by the class; others make a set for each student. Some teachers duplicate them for each student and have the students cut & fold their own. You can cut out just the words and put them in a hat, have each student pick out one word and write the definition and a sentence for that word. Students then swap words and papers, with the next student adding a sentence of his own under the last one. You can have students swap as many times as you like. Each time the student will read the sentences written prior to his own and then add a sentence. You can cut out the words and definitions separately and play "I Have; Who Has?" Each student in the room draws a word and definition. The first student says, "I have (the name of the word). Who has the definition?" The student with the definition reads it then says, "I have (the name of the vocabulary word she has). Who has the definition?" The round continues until all words and definitions have been given.

The View From Saturday Word List

No.	Word	Clue/Definition
1.	ARNOLD	Ginger's understudy
2.	AUGUST	Nadia spends this month with her father.
3.	CALLIGRAPHY	Noah teaches this skill to The Souls.
4.	CARROLL	Author of Alice in Wonderland
5.	CENTURY	Village where Margaret and Izzy live
6.	DIAMONDSTEIN	Izzy's last name
7.	DRAPER	Margaret's last name before marrying Izzy
8.	EPIPHANY	The Souls attended ___ Middle School.
9.	ETHAN	Margaret's grandson
10.	FAIRBAIN	Master of Ceremonies at the district playoffs
11.	FLORIDA	State where Nadia's father lives
12.	GERSHOM	Dr. __: Noah's father; Nadia's mother works for him
13.	GINGER	Nadia's dog
14.	HAM	He takes Julian's book bag.
15.	HOVERING	Nadia's father's new best thing
16.	HYGIENIST	Nadia's mother is a dental ___.
17.	IZZY	Margaret's husband; Nadia's grandfather
18.	KINDNESS	The Souls found this on their journey.
19.	KNAPP	Ham's last name
20.	KORSHAK	Bus driver for Epiphany
21.	LETTER	B & B: a kind of ____ Noah had to write
22.	LUCAS	Ethan's older, perfect brother
23.	MARGARET	Izzy's wife; Ethan's grandmother; former principal
24.	MAXWELL	Epiphany competes against this school on Bowl Day.
25.	MICHAEL	Arnold's owner
26.	MONKEY	Julian's toy symbolizing balance: ivory ___
27.	NOAH	Best man at the wedding
28.	OLINSKI	She selects the Academic Bowl team members.
29.	OPERA	Ethan really enjoyed this performance: Phantom of the ___
30.	PAPER	Nadia had the longest strip of wall ___.
31.	PARAPLEGIC	Word describing Mrs. Olinski's physical condition
32.	PAW	Kind of prints on the wedding invitations
33.	PENNY	Julian magically placed one in the hand of each of The Souls.
34.	POTTER	Ethan or Lucas
35.	PUPPY	Nadia takes this gift to the first tea party
36.	PUZZLE	Gift Ethan takes to the first tea party
37.	ROHMER	District Superintendent of Clarion County
38.	SANDY	Ginger's stage role
39.	SARGASSO	Portion of the North Atlantic where marine life thrives: ___ Sea
40.	SILLINGTON	Tea party location: ___ House
41.	SINGH	Julian's last name
42.	SIXTH	Grade level of the Academic Bowl team students
43.	SOULS	Name of the Academic Bowl team: The ___
44.	TREATS	Ham laced Ginger's with tranquilizers and laxatives
45.	TURTLES	They brought Margaret and Izzy together.
46.	VET	Ham's mother's occupation
47.	WAGON	Noah used his red one to transport things to the clubhouse.
48.	ZATFIG	Term meaning pleasingly plump

The View From Saturday Fill In The Blanks 1

_____ 1. Izzy's last name
_____ 2. Nadia had the longest strip of wall ___.
_____ 3. Village where Margaret and Izzy live
_____ 4. Portion of the North Atlantic where marine life thrives: ___ Sea
_____ 5. Margaret's last name before marrying Izzy
_____ 6. Name of the Academic Bowl team: The ___
_____ 7. Margaret's grandson
_____ 8. Nadia's dog
_____ 9. Nadia's father's new best thing
_____ 10. Nadia spends this month with her father.
_____ 11. Master of Ceremonies at the district playoffs
_____ 12. Ginger's stage role
_____ 13. The Souls found this on their journey.
_____ 14. Ethan's older, perfect brother
_____ 15. Author of Alice in Wonderland
_____ 16. Julian's last name
_____ 17. Kind of prints on the wedding invitations
_____ 18. Margaret's husband; Nadia's grandfather
_____ 19. Julian's toy symbolizing balance: ivory ___
_____ 20. Ginger's understudy

The View From Saturday Fill In The Blanks 1 Answer Key

DIAMONDSTEIN	1. Izzy's last name
PAPER	2. Nadia had the longest strip of wall ___.
CENTURY	3. Village where Margaret and Izzy live
SARGASSO	4. Portion of the North Atlantic where marine life thrives: ___ Sea
DRAPER	5. Margaret's last name before marrying Izzy
SOULS	6. Name of the Academic Bowl team: The ___
ETHAN	7. Margaret's grandson
GINGER	8. Nadia's dog
HOVERING	9. Nadia's father's new best thing
AUGUST	10. Nadia spends this month with her father.
FAIRBAIN	11. Master of Ceremonies at the district playoffs
SANDY	12. Ginger's stage role
KINDNESS	13. The Souls found this on their journey.
LUCAS	14. Ethan's older, perfect brother
CARROLL	15. Author of Alice in Wonderland
SINGH	16. Julian's last name
PAW	17. Kind of prints on the wedding invitations
IZZY	18. Margaret's husband; Nadia's grandfather
MONKEY	19. Julian's toy symbolizing balance: ivory ___
ARNOLD	20. Ginger's understudy

The View From Saturday Fill In The Blanks 2

_____ 1. Margaret's husband; Nadia's grandfather

_____ 2. Margaret's last name before marrying Izzy

_____ 3. The Souls attended ___ Middle School.

_____ 4. Ham's last name

_____ 5. Epiphany competes against this school on Bowl Day.

_____ 6. Grade level of the Academic Bowl team students

_____ 7. Julian magically placed one in the hand of each of The Souls.

_____ 8. Gift Ethan takes to the first tea party

_____ 9. They brought Margaret and Izzy together.

_____ 10. Noah teaches this skill to The Souls.

_____ 11. District Superintendent of Clarion County

_____ 12. Ham's mother's occupation

_____ 13. Julian's last name

_____ 14. Nadia's father's new best thing

_____ 15. Name of the Academic Bowl team: The ___

_____ 16. Izzy's wife; Ethan's grandmother; former principal

_____ 17. B & B: a kind of _____ Noah had to write

_____ 18. Author of Alice in Wonderland

_____ 19. Nadia spends this month with her father.

_____ 20. Term meaning pleasingly plump

The View From Saturday Fill In The Blanks 2 Answer Key

IZZY	1. Margaret's husband; Nadia's grandfather
DRAPER	2. Margaret's last name before marrying Izzy
EPIPHANY	3. The Souls attended ___ Middle School.
KNAPP	4. Ham's last name
MAXWELL	5. Epiphany competes against this school on Bowl Day.
SIXTH	6. Grade level of the Academic Bowl team students
PENNY	7. Julian magically placed one in the hand of each of The Souls.
PUZZLE	8. Gift Ethan takes to the first tea party
TURTLES	9. They brought Margaret and Izzy together.
CALLIGRAPHY	10. Noah teaches this skill to The Souls.
ROHMER	11. District Superintendent of Clarion County
VET	12. Ham's mother's occupation
SINGH	13. Julian's last name
HOVERING	14. Nadia's father's new best thing
SOULS	15. Name of the Academic Bowl team: The ___
MARGARET	16. Izzy's wife; Ethan's grandmother; former principal
LETTER	17. B & B: a kind of _____ Noah had to write
CARROLL	18. Author of Alice in Wonderland
AUGUST	19. Nadia spends this month with her father.
ZATFIG	20. Term meaning pleasingly plump

The View From Saturday Fill In The Blanks 3

_____ 1. Arnold's owner

_____ 2. Ham's mother's occupation

_____ 3. Dr. ___: Noah's father; Nadia's mother works for him

_____ 4. The Souls attended ___ Middle School.

_____ 5. Nadia had the longest strip of wall ___.

_____ 6. Nadia spends this month with her father.

_____ 7. Noah used his red one to transport things to the clubhouse.

_____ 8. Nadia's mother is a dental ___.

_____ 9. Margaret's last name before marrying Izzy

_____ 10. Author of Alice in Wonderland

_____ 11. Ginger's stage role

_____ 12. Margaret's husband; Nadia's grandfather

_____ 13. Tea party location: ___ House

_____ 14. Bus driver for Epiphany

_____ 15. Ethan or Lucas

_____ 16. Ginger's understudy

_____ 17. Gift Ethan takes to the first tea party

_____ 18. The Souls found this on their journey.

_____ 19. Julian's toy symbolizing balance: ivory ___

_____ 20. Name of the Academic Bowl team: The ___

The View From Saturday Fill In The Blanks 3 Answer Key

MICHAEL	1.	Arnold's owner
VET	2.	Ham's mother's occupation
GERSHOM	3.	Dr. __: Noah's father; Nadia's mother works for him
EPIPHANY	4.	The Souls attended ___ Middle School.
PAPER	5.	Nadia had the longest strip of wall ___.
AUGUST	6.	Nadia spends this month with her father.
WAGON	7.	Noah used his red one to transport things to the clubhouse.
HYGIENIST	8.	Nadia's mother is a dental ___.
DRAPER	9.	Margaret's last name before marrying Izzy
CARROLL	10.	Author of Alice in Wonderland
SANDY	11.	Ginger's stage role
IZZY	12.	Margaret's husband; Nadia's grandfather
SILLINGTON	13.	Tea party location: ___ House
KORSHAK	14.	Bus driver for Epiphany
POTTER	15.	Ethan or Lucas
ARNOLD	16.	Ginger's understudy
PUZZLE	17.	Gift Ethan takes to the first tea party
KINDNESS	18.	The Souls found this on their journey.
MONKEY	19.	Julian's toy symbolizing balance: ivory ___
SOULS	20.	Name of the Academic Bowl team: The ___

The View From Saturday Fill In The Blanks 4

_____   1. Julian's toy symbolizing balance: ivory ___
_____   2. District Superintendent of Clarion County
_____   3. Bus driver for Epiphany
_____   4. Name of the Academic Bowl team: The ___
_____   5. The Souls found this on their journey.
_____   6. Ginger's understudy
_____   7. Ham's mother's occupation
_____   8. Izzy's wife; Ethan's grandmother; former principal
_____   9. Margaret's grandson
_____   10. Julian's last name
_____   11. Village where Margaret and Izzy live
_____   12. The Souls attended ___ Middle School.
_____   13. Tea party location: ___ House
_____   14. State where Nadia's father lives
_____   15. Ham laced Ginger's with tranquilizers and laxatives
_____   16. They brought Margaret and Izzy together.
_____   17. Term meaning pleasingly plump
_____   18. Ethan really enjoyed this performance: Phantom of the ___
_____   19. Author of Alice in Wonderland
_____   20. Ethan or Lucas

The View From Saturday Fill In The Blanks 4 Answer Key

MONKEY	1. Julian's toy symbolizing balance: ivory ___
ROHMER	2. District Superintendent of Clarion County
KORSHAK	3. Bus driver for Epiphany
SOULS	4. Name of the Academic Bowl team: The ___
KINDNESS	5. The Souls found this on their journey.
ARNOLD	6. Ginger's understudy
VET	7. Ham's mother's occupation
MARGARET	8. Izzy's wife; Ethan's grandmother; former principal
ETHAN	9. Margaret's grandson
SINGH	10. Julian's last name
CENTURY	11. Village where Margaret and Izzy live
EPIPHANY	12. The Souls attended ___ Middle School.
SILLINGTON	13. Tea party location: ___ House
FLORIDA	14. State where Nadia's father lives
TREATS	15. Ham laced Ginger's with tranquilizers and laxatives
TURTLES	16. They brought Margaret and Izzy together.
ZATFIG	17. Term meaning pleasingly plump
OPERA	18. Ethan really enjoyed this performance: Phantom of the ___
CARROLL	19. Author of Alice in Wonderland
POTTER	20. Ethan or Lucas

The View From Saturday Matching 1

___ 1. OPERA
___ 2. SILLINGTON
___ 3. PUZZLE
___ 4. LETTER
___ 5. KORSHAK
___ 6. ETHAN
___ 7. OLINSKI
___ 8. CARROLL
___ 9. HAM
___10. SANDY
___11. POTTER
___12. SARGASSO
___13. MICHAEL
___14. GERSHOM
___15. DRAPER
___16. ZATFIG
___17. MARGARET
___18. PAPER
___19. FLORIDA
___20. FAIRBAIN
___21. VET
___22. HYGIENIST
___23. ROHMER
___24. KNAPP
___25. SIXTH

A. Master of Ceremonies at the district playoffs
B. Portion of the North Atlantic where marine life thrives: ___ Sea
C. Arnold's owner
D. Izzy's wife; Ethan's grandmother; former principal
E. Author of Alice in Wonderland
F. Nadia's mother is a dental ___.
G. She selects the Academic Bowl team members.
H. Ethan or Lucas
I. Ham's mother's occupation
J. Margaret's grandson
K. Grade level of the Academic Bowl team students
L. Tea party location: ___ House
M. Gift Ethan takes to the first tea party
N. B & B: a kind of ____ Noah had to write
O. Dr. __: Noah's father; Nadia's mother works for him
P. District Superintendent of Clarion County
Q. Ham's last name
R. Margaret's last name before marrying Izzy
S. Ethan really enjoyed this performance: Phantom of the ___
T. Nadia had the longest strip of wall ___.
U. He takes Julian's book bag.
V. Bus driver for Epiphany
W. Term meaning pleasingly plump
X. Ginger's stage role
Y. State where Nadia's father lives

The View From Saturday Matching 1 Answer Key

S - 1.	OPERA	A. Master of Ceremonies at the district playoffs
L - 2.	SILLINGTON	B. Portion of the North Atlantic where marine life thrives: ___ Sea
M - 3.	PUZZLE	C. Arnold's owner
N - 4.	LETTER	D. Izzy's wife; Ethan's grandmother; former principal
V - 5.	KORSHAK	E. Author of Alice in Wonderland
J - 6.	ETHAN	F. Nadia's mother is a dental ___.
G - 7.	OLINSKI	G. She selects the Academic Bowl team members.
E - 8.	CARROLL	H. Ethan or Lucas
U - 9.	HAM	I. Ham's mother's occupation
X - 10.	SANDY	J. Margaret's grandson
H - 11.	POTTER	K. Grade level of the Academic Bowl team students
B - 12.	SARGASSO	L. Tea party location: ___ House
C - 13.	MICHAEL	M. Gift Ethan takes to the first tea party
O - 14.	GERSHOM	N. B & B: a kind of ___ Noah had to write
R - 15.	DRAPER	O. Dr. __: Noah's father; Nadia's mother works for him
W - 16.	ZATFIG	P. District Superintendent of Clarion County
D - 17.	MARGARET	Q. Ham's last name
T - 18.	PAPER	R. Margaret's last name before marrying Izzy
Y - 19.	FLORIDA	S. Ethan really enjoyed this performance: Phantom of the ___
A - 20.	FAIRBAIN	T. Nadia had the longest strip of wall ___.
I - 21.	VET	U. He takes Julian's book bag.
F - 22.	HYGIENIST	V. Bus driver for Epiphany
P - 23.	ROHMER	W. Term meaning pleasingly plump
Q - 24.	KNAPP	X. Ginger's stage role
K - 25.	SIXTH	Y. State where Nadia's father lives

The View From Saturday Matching 2

___ 1. LETTER   A. Ethan's older, perfect brother
___ 2. ZATFIG   B. Ginger's understudy
___ 3. CENTURY   C. Word describing Mrs. Olinski's physical condition
___ 4. SANDY   D. The Souls found this on their journey.
___ 5. MONKEY   E. Term meaning pleasingly plump
___ 6. SOULS   F. Izzy's last name
___ 7. ARNOLD   G. Ethan really enjoyed this performance: Phantom of the ___
___ 8. LUCAS   H. Master of Ceremonies at the district playoffs
___ 9. IZZY   I. Noah used his red one to transport things to the clubhouse.
___10. KNAPP   J. The Souls attended ___ Middle School.
___11. FAIRBAIN   K. Margaret's husband; Nadia's grandfather
___12. VET   L. Julian magically placed one in the hand of each of The Souls.
___13. CALLIGRAPHY   M. Julian's toy symbolizing balance: ivory ___
___14. FLORIDA   N. Gift Ethan takes to the first tea party
___15. PUZZLE   O. Noah teaches this skill to The Souls.
___16. TREATS   P. Grade level of the Academic Bowl team students
___17. DIAMONDSTEIN   Q. Ham's mother's occupation
___18. KORSHAK   R. B & B: a kind of ____ Noah had to write
___19. EPIPHANY   S. Bus driver for Epiphany
___20. WAGON   T. Village where Margaret and Izzy live
___21. PARAPLEGIC   U. Name of the Academic Bowl team: The ___
___22. OPERA   V. Ginger's stage role
___23. PENNY   W. State where Nadia's father lives
___24. KINDNESS   X. Ham laced Ginger's with tranquilizers and laxatives
___25. SIXTH   Y. Ham's last name

The View From Saturday Matching 2 Answer Key

R - 1.	LETTER	A.	Ethan's older, perfect brother
E - 2.	ZATFIG	B.	Ginger's understudy
T - 3.	CENTURY	C.	Word describing Mrs. Olinski's physical condition
V - 4.	SANDY	D.	The Souls found this on their journey.
M - 5.	MONKEY	E.	Term meaning pleasingly plump
U - 6.	SOULS	F.	Izzy's last name
B - 7.	ARNOLD	G.	Ethan really enjoyed this performance: Phantom of the ___
A - 8.	LUCAS	H.	Master of Ceremonies at the district playoffs
K - 9.	IZZY	I.	Noah used his red one to transport things to the clubhouse.
Y -10.	KNAPP	J.	The Souls attended ___ Middle School.
H -11.	FAIRBAIN	K.	Margaret's husband; Nadia's grandfather
Q -12.	VET	L.	Julian magically placed one in the hand of each of The Souls.
O -13.	CALLIGRAPHY	M.	Julian's toy symbolizing balance: ivory ___
W -14.	FLORIDA	N.	Gift Ethan takes to the first tea party
N -15.	PUZZLE	O.	Noah teaches this skill to The Souls.
X -16.	TREATS	P.	Grade level of the Academic Bowl team students
F -17.	DIAMONDSTEIN	Q.	Ham's mother's occupation
S -18.	KORSHAK	R.	B & B: a kind of ____ Noah had to write
J -19.	EPIPHANY	S.	Bus driver for Epiphany
I -20.	WAGON	T.	Village where Margaret and Izzy live
C -21.	PARAPLEGIC	U.	Name of the Academic Bowl team: The ___
G -22.	OPERA	V.	Ginger's stage role
L -23.	PENNY	W.	State where Nadia's father lives
D -24.	KINDNESS	X.	Ham laced Ginger's with tranquilizers and laxatives
P -25.	SIXTH	Y.	Ham's last name

The View From Saturday Matching 3

___ 1. HOVERING   A. Margaret's grandson
___ 2. SANDY   B. Ham laced Ginger's with tranquilizers and laxatives
___ 3. TREATS   C. Grade level of the Academic Bowl team students
___ 4. DRAPER   D. Word describing Mrs. Olinski's physical condition
___ 5. SIXTH   E. Nadia's father's new best thing
___ 6. MONKEY   F. The Souls found this on their journey.
___ 7. ROHMER   G. Nadia's mother is a dental ___.
___ 8. PARAPLEGIC   H. He takes Julian's book bag.
___ 9. KORSHAK   I. Margaret's husband; Nadia's grandfather
___ 10. TURTLES   J. Epiphany competes against this school on Bowl Day.
___ 11. ARNOLD   K. Ethan or Lucas
___ 12. GERSHOM   L. District Superintendent of Clarion County
___ 13. MAXWELL   M. Ham's mother's occupation
___ 14. POTTER   N. Margaret's last name before marrying Izzy
___ 15. MARGARET   O. Julian's toy symbolizing balance: ivory ___
___ 16. SOULS   P. Dr. ___: Noah's father; Nadia's mother works for him
___ 17. VET   Q. Gift Ethan takes to the first tea party
___ 18. HAM   R. Term meaning pleasingly plump
___ 19. ZATFIG   S. Ginger's understudy
___ 20. NOAH   T. Ginger's stage role
___ 21. KINDNESS   U. Bus driver for Epiphany
___ 22. PUZZLE   V. Izzy's wife; Ethan's grandmother; former principal
___ 23. ETHAN   W. Name of the Academic Bowl team: The ___
___ 24. IZZY   X. They brought Margaret and Izzy together.
___ 25. HYGIENIST   Y. Best man at the wedding

The View From Saturday Matching 3 Answer Key

E - 1.	HOVERING	A.	Margaret's grandson
T - 2.	SANDY	B.	Ham laced Ginger's with tranquilizers and laxatives
B - 3.	TREATS	C.	Grade level of the Academic Bowl team students
N - 4.	DRAPER	D.	Word describing Mrs. Olinski's physical condition
C - 5.	SIXTH	E.	Nadia's father's new best thing
O - 6.	MONKEY	F.	The Souls found this on their journey.
L - 7.	ROHMER	G.	Nadia's mother is a dental ___.
D - 8.	PARAPLEGIC	H.	He takes Julian's book bag.
U - 9.	KORSHAK	I.	Margaret's husband; Nadia's grandfather
X - 10.	TURTLES	J.	Epiphany competes against this school on Bowl Day.
S - 11.	ARNOLD	K.	Ethan or Lucas
P - 12.	GERSHOM	L.	District Superintendent of Clarion County
J - 13.	MAXWELL	M.	Ham's mother's occupation
K - 14.	POTTER	N.	Margaret's last name before marrying Izzy
V - 15.	MARGARET	O.	Julian's toy symbolizing balance: ivory ___
W - 16.	SOULS	P.	Dr. ___: Noah's father; Nadia's mother works for him
M - 17.	VET	Q.	Gift Ethan takes to the first tea party
H - 18.	HAM	R.	Term meaning pleasingly plump
R - 19.	ZATFIG	S.	Ginger's understudy
Y - 20.	NOAH	T.	Ginger's stage role
F - 21.	KINDNESS	U.	Bus driver for Epiphany
Q - 22.	PUZZLE	V.	Izzy's wife; Ethan's grandmother; former principal
A - 23.	ETHAN	W.	Name of the Academic Bowl team: The ___
I - 24.	IZZY	X.	They brought Margaret and Izzy together.
G - 25.	HYGIENIST	Y.	Best man at the wedding

The View From Saturday Matching 4

___ 1. EPIPHANY A. Tea party location: ___ House
___ 2. MONKEY B. Nadia's father's new best thing
___ 3. TREATS C. Master of Ceremonies at the district playoffs
___ 4. LETTER D. Dr. __: Noah's father; Nadia's mother works for him
___ 5. OLINSKI E. Ham laced Ginger's with tranquilizers and laxatives
___ 6. LUCAS F. She selects the Academic Bowl team members.
___ 7. SANDY G. Ginger's understudy
___ 8. GERSHOM H. Grade level of the Academic Bowl team students
___ 9. DRAPER I. State where Nadia's father lives
___ 10. HOVERING J. Nadia takes this gift to the first tea party
___ 11. MARGARET K. Julian's toy symbolizing balance: ivory ___
___ 12. SILLINGTON L. Izzy's last name
___ 13. KNAPP M. Margaret's last name before marrying Izzy
___ 14. CENTURY N. He takes Julian's book bag.
___ 15. SINGH O. B & B: a kind of ____ Noah had to write
___ 16. ARNOLD P. Julian's last name
___ 17. SIXTH Q. Nadia had the longest strip of wall ___.
___ 18. VET R. Ham's last name
___ 19. DIAMONDSTEIN S. Village where Margaret and Izzy live
___ 20. FAIRBAIN T. Ginger's stage role
___ 21. HAM U. Ethan or Lucas
___ 22. FLORIDA V. Izzy's wife; Ethan's grandmother; former principal
___ 23. PAPER W. Ethan's older, perfect brother
___ 24. POTTER X. The Souls attended ___ Middle School.
___ 25. PUPPY Y. Ham's mother's occupation

The View From Saturday Matching 4 Answer Key

X - 1. EPIPHANY	A.	Tea party location: ___ House
K - 2. MONKEY	B.	Nadia's father's new best thing
E - 3. TREATS	C.	Master of Ceremonies at the district playoffs
O - 4. LETTER	D.	Dr. __: Noah's father; Nadia's mother works for him
F - 5. OLINSKI	E.	Ham laced Ginger's with tranquilizers and laxatives
W - 6. LUCAS	F.	She selects the Academic Bowl team members.
T - 7. SANDY	G.	Ginger's understudy
D - 8. GERSHOM	H.	Grade level of the Academic Bowl team students
M - 9. DRAPER	I.	State where Nadia's father lives
B - 10. HOVERING	J.	Nadia takes this gift to the first tea party
V - 11. MARGARET	K.	Julian's toy symbolizing balance: ivory ___
A - 12. SILLINGTON	L.	Izzy's last name
R - 13. KNAPP	M.	Margaret's last name before marrying Izzy
S - 14. CENTURY	N.	He takes Julian's book bag.
P - 15. SINGH	O.	B & B: a kind of ____ Noah had to write
G - 16. ARNOLD	P.	Julian's last name
H - 17. SIXTH	Q.	Nadia had the longest strip of wall ___.
Y - 18. VET	R.	Ham's last name
L - 19. DIAMONDSTEIN	S.	Village where Margaret and Izzy live
C - 20. FAIRBAIN	T.	Ginger's stage role
N - 21. HAM	U.	Ethan or Lucas
I - 22. FLORIDA	V.	Izzy's wife; Ethan's grandmother; former principal
Q - 23. PAPER	W.	Ethan's older, perfect brother
U - 24. POTTER	X.	The Souls attended ___ Middle School.
J - 25. PUPPY	Y.	Ham's mother's occupation

The View From Saturday Magic Squares 1

Match the definition with the vocabulary word. Put your answers in the magic squares below. When your answers are correct, all columns and rows will add to the same number.

A. TREATS
B. IZZY
C. WAGON
D. PARAPLEGIC
E. VET
F. MAXWELL
G. SILLINGTON
H. CALLIGRAPHY
I. ARNOLD
J. PAW
K. ROHMER
L. HAM
M. LUCAS
N. PAPER
O. CENTURY
P. ETHAN

1. Margaret's husband; Nadia's grandfather
2. Tea party location: ___ House
3. District Superintendent of Clarion County
4. Nadia had the longest strip of wall ___.
5. Ethan's older, perfect brother
6. He takes Julian's book bag.
7. Noah teaches this skill to The Souls.
8. Ham laced Ginger's with tranquilizers and laxatives
9. Margaret's grandson
10. Ginger's understudy
11. Ham's mother's occupation
12. Word describing Mrs. Olinski's physical condition
13. Noah used his red one to transport things to the clubhouse.
14. Epiphany competes against this school on Bowl Day.
15. Kind of prints on the wedding invitations
16. Village where Margaret and Izzy live

A=	B=	C=	D=
E=	F=	G=	H=
I=	J=	K=	L=
M=	N=	O=	P=

The View From Saturday Magic Squares 1 Answer Key

Match the definition with the vocabulary word. Put your answers in the magic squares below. When your answers are correct, all columns and rows will add to the same number.

A. TREATS
B. IZZY
C. WAGON
D. PARAPLEGIC
E. VET
F. MAXWELL
G. SILLINGTON
H. CALLIGRAPHY
I. ARNOLD
J. PAW
K. ROHMER
L. HAM
M. LUCAS
N. PAPER
O. CENTURY
P. ETHAN

1. Margaret's husband; Nadia's grandfather
2. Tea party location: ___ House
3. District Superintendent of Clarion County
4. Nadia had the longest strip of wall ___.
5. Ethan's older, perfect brother
6. He takes Julian's book bag.
7. Noah teaches this skill to The Souls.
8. Ham laced Ginger's with tranquilizers and laxatives
9. Margaret's grandson
10. Ginger's understudy
11. Ham's mother's occupation
12. Word describing Mrs. Olinski's physical condition
13. Noah used his red one to transport things to the clubhouse.
14. Epiphany competes against this school on Bowl Day.
15. Kind of prints on the wedding invitations
16. Village where Margaret and Izzy live

A=8	B=1	C=13	D=12
E=11	F=14	G=2	H=7
I=10	J=15	K=3	L=6
M=5	N=4	O=16	P=9

The View From Saturday Magic Squares 2

Match the definition with the vocabulary word. Put your answers in the magic squares below. When your answers are correct, all columns and rows will add to the same number.

A. PAW   E. CENTURY   I. WAGON   M. KORSHAK
B. HAM   F. KINDNESS   J. MONKEY   N. SOULS
C. ETHAN   G. TREATS   K. VET   O. EPIPHANY
D. PAPER   H. POTTER   L. PARAPLEGIC   P. TURTLES

1. Bus driver for Epiphany
2. The Souls found this on their journey.
3. Ethan or Lucas
4. The Souls attended ___ Middle School.
5. Word describing Mrs. Olinski's physical condition
6. Margaret's grandson
7. Kind of prints on the wedding invitations
8. Julian's toy symbolizing balance: ivory ___
9. Ham's mother's occupation
10. Nadia had the longest strip of wall ___.
11. He takes Julian's book bag.
12. Noah used his red one to transport things to the clubhouse.
13. Name of the Academic Bowl team: The ___
14. Village where Margaret and Izzy live
15. Ham laced Ginger's with tranquilizers and laxatives
16. They brought Margaret and Izzy together.

A=	B=	C=	D=
E=	F=	G=	H=
I=	J=	K=	L=
M=	N=	O=	P=

The View From Saturday Magic Squares 2 Answer Key

Match the definition with the vocabulary word. Put your answers in the magic squares below. When your answers are correct, all columns and rows will add to the same number.

A. PAW
B. HAM
C. ETHAN
D. PAPER
E. CENTURY
F. KINDNESS
G. TREATS
H. POTTER
I. WAGON
J. MONKEY
K. VET
L. PARAPLEGIC
M. KORSHAK
N. SOULS
O. EPIPHANY
P. TURTLES

1. Bus driver for Epiphany
2. The Souls found this on their journey.
3. Ethan or Lucas
4. The Souls attended ___ Middle School.
5. Word describing Mrs. Olinski's physical condition
6. Margaret's grandson
7. Kind of prints on the wedding invitations
8. Julian's toy symbolizing balance: ivory ___
9. Ham's mother's occupation
10. Nadia had the longest strip of wall ___.
11. He takes Julian's book bag.
12. Noah used his red one to transport things to the clubhouse.
13. Name of the Academic Bowl team: The ___
14. Village where Margaret and Izzy live
15. Ham laced Ginger's with tranquilizers and laxatives
16. They brought Margaret and Izzy together.

A=7	B=11	C=6	D=10
E=14	F=2	G=15	H=3
I=12	J=8	K=9	L=5
M=1	N=13	O=4	P=16

The View From Saturday Magic Squares 3

Match the definition with the vocabulary word. Put your answers in the magic squares below. When your answers are correct, all columns and rows will add to the same number.

A. IZZY
B. CARROLL
C. KNAPP
D. KINDNESS
E. PAW
F. MICHAEL
G. SINGH
H. CALLIGRAPHY
I. LETTER
J. NOAH
K. PARAPLEGIC
L. HAM
M. MONKEY
N. FAIRBAIN
O. GERSHOM
P. CENTURY

1. Arnold's owner
2. B & B: a kind of ____ Noah had to write
3. Dr. __: Noah's father; Nadia's mother works for him
4. The Souls found this on their journey.
5. Julian's toy symbolizing balance: ivory ____
6. Author of Alice in Wonderland
7. Noah teaches this skill to The Souls.
8. Word describing Mrs. Olinski's physical condition
9. Ham's last name
10. Village where Margaret and Izzy live
11. Best man at the wedding
12. Kind of prints on the wedding invitations
13. He takes Julian's book bag.
14. Julian's last name
15. Margaret's husband; Nadia's grandfather
16. Master of Ceremonies at the district playoffs

A=	B=	C=	D=
E=	F=	G=	H=
I=	J=	K=	L=
M=	N=	O=	P=

The View From Saturday Magic Squares 3 Answer Key

Match the definition with the vocabulary word. Put your answers in the magic squares below. When your answers are correct, all columns and rows will add to the same number.

A. IZZY
B. CARROLL
C. KNAPP
D. KINDNESS
E. PAW
F. MICHAEL
G. SINGH
H. CALLIGRAPHY
I. LETTER
J. NOAH
K. PARAPLEGIC
L. HAM
M. MONKEY
N. FAIRBAIN
O. GERSHOM
P. CENTURY

1. Arnold's owner
2. B & B: a kind of ____ Noah had to write
3. Dr. __: Noah's father; Nadia's mother works for him
4. The Souls found this on their journey.
5. Julian's toy symbolizing balance: ivory ___
6. Author of Alice in Wonderland
7. Noah teaches this skill to The Souls.
8. Word describing Mrs. Olinski's physical condition
9. Ham's last name
10. Village where Margaret and Izzy live
11. Best man at the wedding
12. Kind of prints on the wedding invitations
13. He takes Julian's book bag.
14. Julian's last name
15. Margaret's husband; Nadia's grandfather
16. Master of Ceremonies at the district playoffs

A=15	B=6	C=9	D=4
E=12	F=1	G=14	H=7
I=2	J=11	K=8	L=13
M=5	N=16	O=3	P=10

The View From Saturday Magic Squares 4

Match the definition with the vocabulary word. Put your answers in the magic squares below. When your answers are correct, all columns and rows will add to the same number.

A. CENTURY
B. PUPPY
C. PAPER
D. PENNY
E. TURTLES
F. OPERA
G. ETHAN
H. SILLINGTON
I. WAGON
J. SANDY
K. HOVERING
L. KINDNESS
M. PARAPLEGIC
N. IZZY
O. MAXWELL
P. DRAPER

1. Tea party location: ___ House
2. Word describing Mrs. Olinski's physical condition
3. Nadia takes this gift to the first tea party
4. Nadia's father's new best thing
5. Ginger's stage role
6. Nadia had the longest strip of wall ___.
7. Margaret's last name before marrying Izzy
8. They brought Margaret and Izzy together.
9. Epiphany competes against this school on Bowl Day.
10. Ethan really enjoyed this performance: Phantom of the ___
11. Noah used his red one to transport things to the clubhouse.
12. Julian magically placed one in the hand of each of The Souls.
13. Village where Margaret and Izzy live
14. The Souls found this on their journey.
15. Margaret's grandson
16. Margaret's husband; Nadia's grandfather

A=	B=	C=	D=
E=	F=	G=	H=
I=	J=	K=	L=
M=	N=	O=	P=

27
Copyrighted

The View From Saturday Magic Squares 4 Answer Key

Match the definition with the vocabulary word. Put your answers in the magic squares below. When your answers are correct, all columns and rows will add to the same number.

A. CENTURY
B. PUPPY
C. PAPER
D. PENNY
E. TURTLES
F. OPERA
G. ETHAN
H. SILLINGTON
I. WAGON
J. SANDY
K. HOVERING
L. KINDNESS
M. PARAPLEGIC
N. IZZY
O. MAXWELL
P. DRAPER

1. Tea party location: ___ House
2. Word describing Mrs. Olinski's physical condition
3. Nadia takes this gift to the first tea party
4. Nadia's father's new best thing
5. Ginger's stage role
6. Nadia had the longest strip of wall ___.
7. Margaret's last name before marrying Izzy
8. They brought Margaret and Izzy together.
9. Epiphany competes against this school on Bowl Day.
10. Ethan really enjoyed this performance: Phantom of the ___
11. Noah used his red one to transport things to the clubhouse.
12. Julian magically placed one in the hand of each of The Souls.
13. Village where Margaret and Izzy live
14. The Souls found this on their journey.
15. Margaret's grandson
16. Margaret's husband; Nadia's grandfather

A=13	B=3	C=6	D=12
E=8	F=10	G=15	H=1
I=11	J=5	K=4	L=14
M=2	N=16	O=9	P=7

The View From Saturday Word Search 1

```
N L H Y G I E N I S T M P U Z Z L E B Q
C O T H I M L L E W X E I D R A P E R K
P F A R N W H G F T N P V C D Z S H O B
F X L H G H N H S N H D K P H H T W L Q
I T Z O E I N T Y Y V A M Y R A A L I H
R Z G V R S X D I A M O N D S T E I N L
G J Z E O I Q K Z R M A S I Y W R L S T
P D V Y H N D N Z A H T L A X G T C K D
S O W B M G R A H P S L Q A N S N J I Y
H A N L E H T P I U I W M O E D S W H W
P S R G R F H P G N S H G L D K Y P C J
L S J G I H E U G C K A T Y L O A G A P
V E T G A D A T M E W R B H K R S E R C
P N T P S S O M A N U E T C G S O R R P
P D P T U N S Q R T N P S I V H U S O R
P N L O E P N O G U Q O L I T A L H L P
K I B Y T R P H A R N L U F X K S O L T
P K Q F T T F Y R Y A S C B C T J M Q V
A R N O L D E S E C J R A G D S H K C G
M O N K E Y D R T H R H S P A P E R G P
```

Arnold's owner (7)
Author of Alice in Wonderland (7)
B & B: a kind of ____ Noah had to write (6)
Best man at the wedding (4)
Bus driver for Epiphany (7)
District Superintendent of Clarion County (6)
Dr. __: Noah's father; Nadia's mother works for him (7)
Epiphany competes against this school on Bowl Day. (7)
Ethan or Lucas (6)
Ethan really enjoyed this performance: Phantom of the ___ (5)
Ethan's older, perfect brother (5)
Gift Ethan takes to the first tea party (6)
Ginger's stage role (5)
Ginger's understudy (6)
Grade level of the Academic Bowl team students (5)
Ham laced Ginger's with tranquilizers and laxatives (6)
Ham's last name (5)
Ham's mother's occupation (3)
He takes Julian's book bag. (3)
Izzy's last name (12)
Izzy's wife; Ethan's grandmother; former principal (8)
Julian magically placed one in the hand of each of

The Souls. (5)
Julian's last name (5)
Julian's toy symbolizing balance: ivory ___ (6)
Kind of prints on the wedding invitations (3)
Margaret's grandson (5)
Margaret's husband; Nadia's grandfather (4)
Margaret's last name before marrying Izzy (6)
Nadia had the longest strip of wall ___. (5)
Nadia spends this month with her father. (6)
Nadia takes this gift to the first tea party (5)
Nadia's dog (6)
Nadia's father's new best thing (8)
Nadia's mother is a dental ___. (9)
Name of the Academic Bowl team: The ___ (5)
Noah teaches this skill to The Souls. (11)
Noah used his red one to transport things to the clubhouse. (5)
Portion of the North Atlantic where marine life thrives: ___ Sea (8)
She selects the Academic Bowl team members. (7)
State where Nadia's father lives (7)
Tea party location: ___ House (10)
Term meaning pleasingly plump (6)
The Souls attended ___ Middle School. (8)
The Souls found this on their journey. (8)
They brought Margaret and Izzy together. (7)
Village where Margaret and Izzy live (7)

The View From Saturday Word Search 1 Answer Key

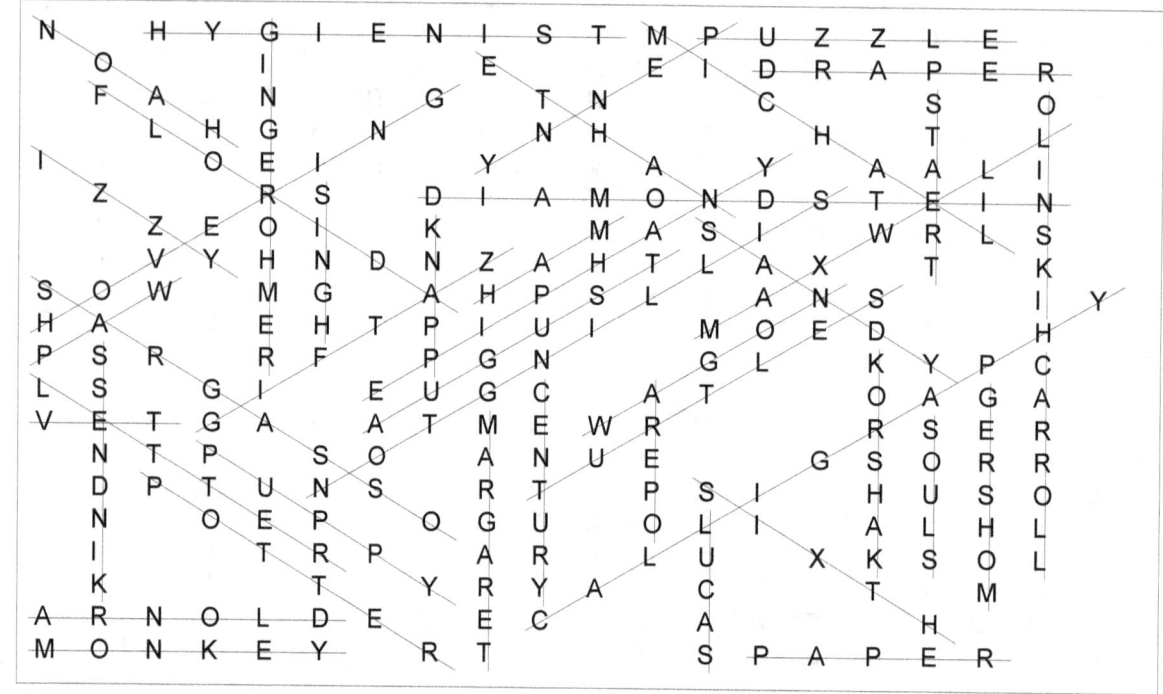

Arnold's owner (7)
Author of Alice in Wonderland (7)
B & B: a kind of ____ Noah had to write (6)
Best man at the wedding (4)
Bus driver for Epiphany (7)
District Superintendent of Clarion County (6)
Dr. __: Noah's father; Nadia's mother works for him (7)
Epiphany competes against this school on Bowl Day. (7)
Ethan or Lucas (6)
Ethan really enjoyed this performance: Phantom of the ___ (5)
Ethan's older, perfect brother (5)
Gift Ethan takes to the first tea party (6)
Ginger's stage role (5)
Ginger's understudy (6)
Grade level of the Academic Bowl team students (5)
Ham laced Ginger's with tranquilizers and laxatives (6)
Ham's last name (5)
Ham's mother's occupation (3)
He takes Julian's book bag. (3)
Izzy's last name (12)
Izzy's wife; Ethan's grandmother; former principal (8)
Julian magically placed one in the hand of each of The Souls. (5)
Julian's last name (5)
Julian's toy symbolizing balance: ivory ___ (6)
Kind of prints on the wedding invitations (3)
Margaret's grandson (5)
Margaret's husband; Nadia's grandfather (4)
Margaret's last name before marrying Izzy (6)
Nadia had the longest strip of wall ___. (5)
Nadia spends this month with her father. (6)
Nadia takes this gift to the first tea party (5)
Nadia's dog (6)
Nadia's father's new best thing (8)
Nadia's mother is a dental ___. (9)
Name of the Academic Bowl team: The ___ (5)
Noah teaches this skill to The Souls. (11)
Noah used his red one to transport things to the clubhouse. (5)
Portion of the North Atlantic where marine life thrives: ___ Sea (8)
She selects the Academic Bowl team members. (7)
State where Nadia's father lives (7)
Tea party location: ___ House (10)
Term meaning pleasingly plump (6)
The Souls attended ___ Middle School. (8)
The Souls found this on their journey. (8)
They brought Margaret and Izzy together. (7)
Village where Margaret and Izzy live (7)

The View From Saturday Word Search 2

```
X X S B L X M S H P P M F G P Q F P D Z
J Q D O Q O B D I D O Q G N R L A R P G
P X F S H Q F X H X T B F O P T I Y L L
P Q S S B A U G U S T D R A P E R S B C
B A R A D C N P E R E H P H P U B O X G
V E W G D I H L E Q R E N I T F A U Z Z
G N Y R S Z T A N C R A P N D N I L S F
S O H A S R T D Y Y H H E L F V N S M W
M L F S U S M I L T A C O T Z T E G A L
N I B T K M O R E N N N P Y Z N I H X Y
K N C J J S N O Y P R Z H Y D F V A W G
N S D H A Y K L R A U P Z N T L E M E X
A K G C A B E F V X A Z I A C Q T N L K
P I U R L E Y L P R I K Z K B W N O L G
P L K G W E L W G E R S A L C Z Q G Q Z
U S Y G I O T I M E N H B C E G H A S Y
P R D W R N L T M S S N X D J K R W D J
P F N R C L G H E R N H Y G I E N I S T
Y S A V A Q O E O R P A R A P L E G I C
F C S C Q R J K R X J G H O V E R I N G
```

Arnold's owner (7)
Author of Alice in Wonderland (7)
B & B: a kind of ____ Noah had to write (6)
Best man at the wedding (4)
Bus driver for Epiphany (7)
District Superintendent of Clarion County (6)
Dr. __: Noah's father; Nadia's mother works for him (7)
Epiphany competes against this school on Bowl Day. (7)
Ethan or Lucas (6)
Ethan really enjoyed this performance: Phantom of the ___ (5)
Ethan's older, perfect brother (5)
Gift Ethan takes to the first tea party (6)
Ginger's stage role (5)
Ginger's understudy (6)
Grade level of the Academic Bowl team students (5)
Ham laced Ginger's with tranquilizers and laxatives (6)
Ham's last name (5)
Ham's mother's occupation (3)
He takes Julian's book bag. (3)
Julian magically placed one in the hand of each of The Souls. (5)
Julian's last name (5)
Julian's toy symbolizing balance: ivory ___ (6)
Kind of prints on the wedding invitations (3)
Margaret's grandson (5)
Margaret's husband; Nadia's grandfather (4)
Margaret's last name before marrying Izzy (6)
Master of Ceremonies at the district playoffs (8)
Nadia had the longest strip of wall ___. (5)
Nadia spends this month with her father. (6)
Nadia takes this gift to the first tea party (5)
Nadia's dog (6)
Nadia's father's new best thing (8)
Nadia's mother is a dental ___. (9)
Name of the Academic Bowl team: The ___ (5)
Noah teaches this skill to The Souls. (11)
Noah used his red one to transport things to the clubhouse. (5)
Portion of the North Atlantic where marine life thrives: ___ Sea (8)
She selects the Academic Bowl team members. (7)
State where Nadia's father lives (7)
Term meaning pleasingly plump (6)
The Souls attended ___ Middle School. (8)
The Souls found this on their journey. (8)
They brought Margaret and Izzy together. (7)
Village where Margaret and Izzy live (7)
Word describing Mrs. Olinski's physical condition (10)

The View From Saturday Word Search 2 Answer Key

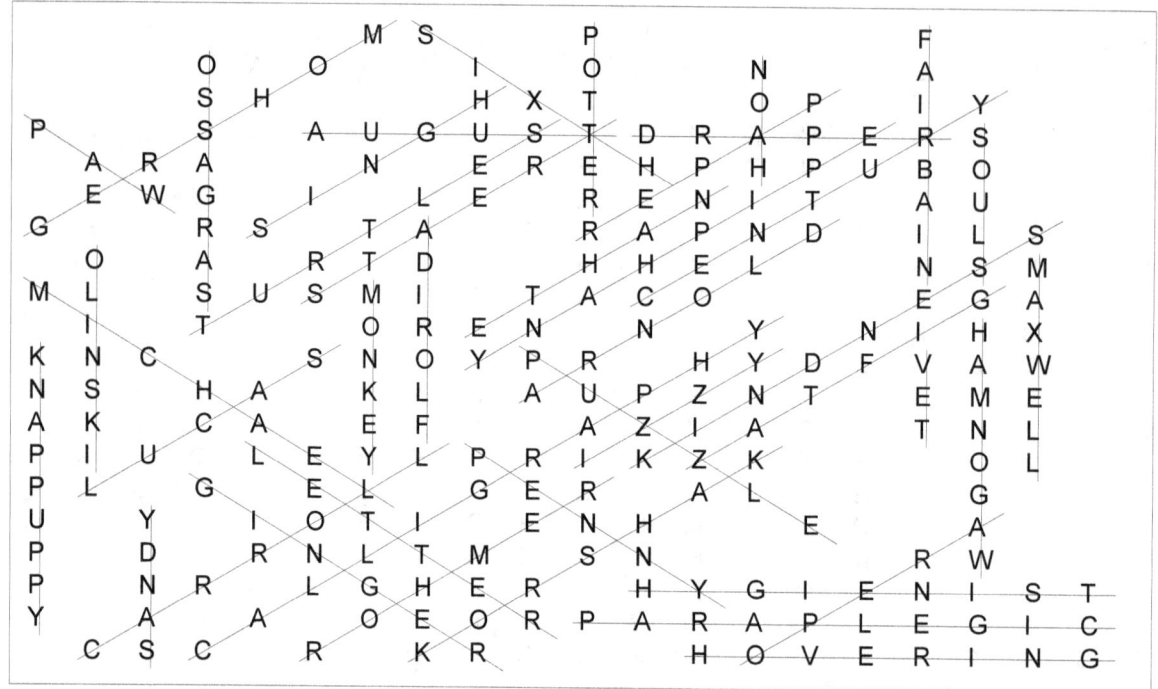

Arnold's owner (7)
Author of Alice in Wonderland (7)
B & B: a kind of ____ Noah had to write (6)
Best man at the wedding (4)
Bus driver for Epiphany (7)
District Superintendent of Clarion County (6)
Dr. __: Noah's father; Nadia's mother works for him (7)
Epiphany competes against this school on Bowl Day. (7)
Ethan or Lucas (6)
Ethan really enjoyed this performance: Phantom of the ___ (5)
Ethan's older, perfect brother (5)
Gift Ethan takes to the first tea party (6)
Ginger's stage role (5)
Ginger's understudy (6)
Grade level of the Academic Bowl team students (5)
Ham laced Ginger's with tranquilizers and laxatives (6)
Ham's last name (5)
Ham's mother's occupation (3)
He takes Julian's book bag. (3)
Julian magically placed one in the hand of each of The Souls. (5)
Julian's last name (5)
Julian's toy symbolizing balance: ivory ___ (6)

Kind of prints on the wedding invitations (3)
Margaret's grandson (5)
Margaret's husband; Nadia's grandfather (4)
Margaret's last name before marrying Izzy (6)
Master of Ceremonies at the district playoffs (8)
Nadia had the longest strip of wall ___. (5)
Nadia spends this month with her father. (6)
Nadia takes this gift to the first tea party (5)
Nadia's dog (6)
Nadia's father's new best thing (8)
Nadia's mother is a dental ___. (9)
Name of the Academic Bowl team: The ___ (5)
Noah teaches this skill to The Souls. (11)
Noah used his red one to transport things to the clubhouse. (5)
Portion of the North Atlantic where marine life thrives: ___ Sea (8)
She selects the Academic Bowl team members. (7)
State where Nadia's father lives (7)
Term meaning pleasingly plump (6)
The Souls attended ___ Middle School. (8)
The Souls found this on their journey. (8)
They brought Margaret and Izzy together. (7)
Village where Margaret and Izzy live (7)
Word describing Mrs. Olinski's physical condition (10)

The View From Saturday Word Search 3

```
S P M P Q T N P Y R T S J T T F E K J Z
S N P E S Y M O B B U W R F Y M T Y G Y
A R K N D J D M A C R Y A T X W H Q E Y
U S J N O G A W P H T K O R S H A K L B
G G A Y A H P S U Y L B Q I N M N L U P
U S L D M P D I P G E M L M M O E T C V
S P P I D D P X P I S L J M W L Y A K
T R E A T S V T Y E I G B C X G S D S W
C E B M R D N H H N R N E A H S P I A L
V G F O E A B M G I V I M R Y A N C R K
E N L N P M P T S S X R E L S G E G X
T I O D A P O L S T P E P K H T L A R
S G R S R N C H E H Q V I N F T O V S B
N D I T D K B R N G G O P H E M F M S P
L P D E H V M G D T I H H L Y W Z X O Y
D G A I Z Z Y H N P P C A C E N T U R Y
B T G N N F V M I A U D N Y F R H G V K
J F T X Z D A N K W Y Z Y N W E R Q O G
T S K X X H V A I C D F H Z S C P G Q L J
P O T T E R A A G R A M Y G L Z A T F I G
D N X M E C P H O B R L S C E P Z F N S
B G M P D Y W P H M A R L F F P S F S L
W B O X S W D H M R K I O L B N W V K V
D H S O U L S R P S J N L N K P B I K
F K C A L L I G R A P H Y M L K N G J V
```

ARNOLD	FLORIDA	LETTER	PARAPLEGIC	SINGH
AUGUST	GERSHOM	LUCAS	PAW	SIXTH
CALLIGRAPHY	GINGER	MARGARET	PENNY	SOULS
CARROLL	HAM	MAXWELL	POTTER	TREATS
CENTURY	HOVERING	MICHAEL	PUPPY	TURTLES
DIAMONDSTEIN	HYGIENIST	MONKEY	PUZZLE	VET
DRAPER	IZZY	NOAH	ROHMER	WAGON
EPIPHANY	KINDNESS	OLINSKI	SANDY	ZATFIG
ETHAN	KNAPP	OPERA	SARGASSO	
FAIRBAIN	KORSHAK	PAPER	SILLINGTON	

The View From Saturday Word Search 3 Answer Key

ARNOLD	FLORIDA	LETTER	PARAPLEGIC	SINGH
AUGUST	GERSHOM	LUCAS	PAW	SIXTH
CALLIGRAPHY	GINGER	MARGARET	PENNY	SOULS
CARROLL	HAM	MAXWELL	POTTER	TREATS
CENTURY	HOVERING	MICHAEL	PUPPY	TURTLES
DIAMONDSTEIN	HYGIENIST	MONKEY	PUZZLE	VET
DRAPER	IZZY	NOAH	ROHMER	WAGON
EPIPHANY	KINDNESS	OLINSKI	SANDY	ZATFIG
ETHAN	KNAPP	OPERA	SARGASSO	
FAIRBAIN	KORSHAK	PAPER	SILLINGTON	

The View From Saturday Word Search 4

```
P F K S G S D X G B B C K K Z G C R H F
Y M P L T S S V L T S B Q Y J A E M H V
F A I R B S I N K Z G W Y P C P T Q B Q
K N O T G N I L L I S Y D N A S R F Q S
S Y P K D V K E G E Z R Q P R W E W I Z
H I E S I A W J Z T U O L R V P M G G
J C N J J H A D I T B T P N O G A W E Q
V L N G C D N M J S C N E B L H R M R G
C Y Y I H Z M X O I J E R R L C D O S M
R X M J C W S B N N L C A S K M C N H C
S S N A H T E A Y P E D P O T T E R K O L
M I B O U W L Y R I G S U C M T O E M V
A C X Y A G D T Y G Q Y T P R L H Y K X
X K H T D H U Q V Y A T K E P K M H F X
W C N G H R P S N H E S A F I Y E P P L
E J L A T F C A T V F S S X C N R A H Q
L F S L P G H T B S S T B O M K G R S K
L G E M W P A R A P D X Q R G I C I Q G H
W S T S I P Z C D X Q R N Z N N H I S Y
C H N P H W U C I H H A B G H D G L F Y
P N E W J L R L R S V G E C W N L T C
O L I N S K I H O V E R I N G E P A Q N
A R N O L D H U L S C A M J X S Z C N H
P U Z Z L E L S F R J M M H Z S M V Q J
H P K O R S H A K Z Y B K Y V B X J D Y
```

ARNOLD	FLORIDA	LETTER	PARAPLEGIC	SINGH
AUGUST	GERSHOM	LUCAS	PAW	SIXTH
CALLIGRAPHY	GINGER	MARGARET	PENNY	SOULS
CARROLL	HAM	MAXWELL	POTTER	TREATS
CENTURY	HOVERING	MICHAEL	PUPPY	TURTLES
DIAMONDSTEIN	HYGIENIST	MONKEY	PUZZLE	VET
DRAPER	IZZY	NOAH	ROHMER	WAGON
EPIPHANY	KINDNESS	OLINSKI	SANDY	ZATFIG
ETHAN	KNAPP	OPERA	SARGASSO	
FAIRBAIN	KORSHAK	PAPER	SILLINGTON	

The View From Saturday Word Search 4 Answer Key

ARNOLD	FLORIDA	LETTER	PARAPLEGIC	SINGH
AUGUST	GERSHOM	LUCAS	PAW	SIXTH
CALLIGRAPHY	GINGER	MARGARET	PENNY	SOULS
CARROLL	HAM	MAXWELL	POTTER	TREATS
CENTURY	HOVERING	MICHAEL	PUPPY	TURTLES
DIAMONDSTEIN	HYGIENIST	MONKEY	PUZZLE	VET
DRAPER	IZZY	NOAH	ROHMER	WAGON
EPIPHANY	KINDNESS	OLINSKI	SANDY	ZATFIG
ETHAN	KNAPP	OPERA	SARGASSO	
FAIRBAIN	KORSHAK	PAPER	SILLINGTON	

The View From Saturday Crossword 1

Across
1. Izzy's last name
6. Kind of prints on the wedding invitations
8. Ethan really enjoyed this performance: Phantom of the ___
9. Nadia's mother is a dental ___.
12. Julian's toy symbolizing balance: ivory ___
14. Julian magically placed one in the hand of each of The Souls.
15. Ham's mother's occupation
16. Portion of the North Atlantic where marine life thrives: ___ Sea
19. Ethan's older, perfect brother
22. Ham laced Ginger's with tranquilizers and laxatives
24. Nadia spends this month with her father.
25. Nadia takes this gift to the first tea party
26. Author of Alice in Wonderland

Down
2. Margaret's husband; Nadia's grandfather
3. They brought Margaret and Izzy together.
4. Best man at the wedding
5. B & B: a kind of ____ Noah had to write
6. Word describing Mrs. Olinski's physical condition
7. Noah used his red one to transport things to the clubhouse.
9. He takes Julian's book bag.
10. Nadia's dog
11. Ham's last name
13. Margaret's grandson
16. Julian's last name
17. Grade level of the Academic Bowl team students
18. She selects the Academic Bowl team members.
20. Ginger's understudy
21. Margaret's last name before marrying Izzy
23. Nadia had the longest strip of wall ___.

The View From Saturday Crossword 1 Answer Key

	1 D	2 I	A	M	O	N	D	3 S	T	4 E	I	N		5 L		6 P	A	7 W
		Z						U				8 O	P	E	R	A		A
		Z						R		A				T		R		G
	9 H	10 G	I	E	N	I	S	T		H				T		A		O
	A		I					L		11 K				E		P		N
	12 M	O	N	K	13 E	Y		14 P	E	N	N	Y		R		L		
			G		T			S		A				15 V	E	T		
			E		H					P				G				
	16 S	A	R	G	A	S	17 S	O				18 P		O		I		
	I				N		I							19 L	U	C	20 A	S
	N		21 D				X							I			R	
	G		22 T	R	E	A	T	S		23 P				N			N	
	H		A				H			24 A	U	G	U	S	T		O	
			25 P	U	P	P	Y			P				K			L	
			E							E				I			D	
	26 C	A	R	R	O	L	L			R								

Across

1. Izzy's last name
6. Kind of prints on the wedding invitations
8. Ethan really enjoyed this performance: Phantom of the ___
9. Nadia's mother is a dental ___.
12. Julian's toy symbolizing balance: ivory ___
14. Julian magically placed one in the hand of each of The Souls.
15. Ham's mother's occupation
16. Portion of the North Atlantic where marine life thrives: ___ Sea
19. Ethan's older, perfect brother
22. Ham laced Ginger's with tranquilizers and laxatives
24. Nadia spends this month with her father.
25. Nadia takes this gift to the first tea party
26. Author of Alice in Wonderland

Down

2. Margaret's husband; Nadia's grandfather
3. They brought Margaret and Izzy together.
4. Best man at the wedding
5. B & B: a kind of ____ Noah had to write
6. Word describing Mrs. Olinski's physical condition
7. Noah used his red one to transport things to the clubhouse.
9. He takes Julian's book bag.
10. Nadia's dog
11. Ham's last name
13. Margaret's grandson
16. Julian's last name
17. Grade level of the Academic Bowl team students
18. She selects the Academic Bowl team members.
20. Ginger's understudy
21. Margaret's last name before marrying Izzy
23. Nadia had the longest strip of wall ___.

The View From Saturday Crossword 2

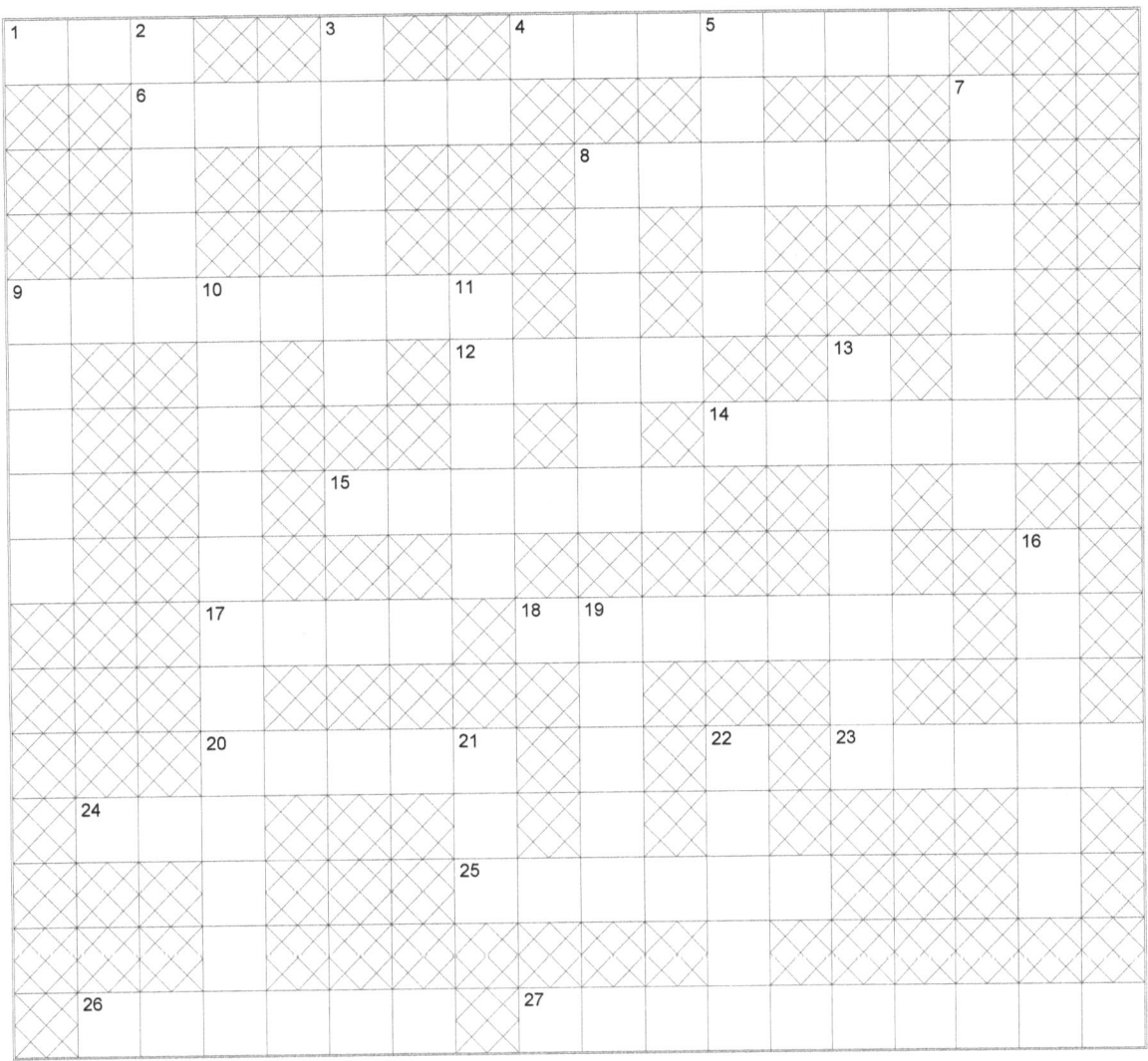

Across
1. Kind of prints on the wedding invitations
4. Bus driver for Epiphany
6. Ginger's understudy
8. Julian magically placed one in the hand of each of The Souls.
9. The Souls found this on their journey.
12. Margaret's husband; Nadia's grandfather
14. Margaret's last name before marrying Izzy
15. B & B: a kind of ____ Noah had to write
17. Best man at the wedding
18. Dr. __: Noah's father; Nadia's mother works for him
20. Julian's last name
23. Ethan's older, perfect brother
24. Ham's mother's occupation
25. Julian's toy symbolizing balance: ivory ___
26. Nadia's dog
27. Word describing Mrs. Olinski's physical condition

Down
2. Noah used his red one to transport things to the clubhouse.
3. District Superintendent of Clarion County
5. Ginger's stage role
7. Arnold's owner
8. Gift Ethan takes to the first tea party
9. Ham's last name
10. Izzy's last name
11. Grade level of the Academic Bowl team students
13. Author of Alice in Wonderland
16. Ham laced Ginger's with tranquilizers and laxatives
19. Margaret's grandson
21. He takes Julian's book bag.
22. Ethan really enjoyed this performance: Phantom of the ___

The View From Saturday Crossword 2 Answer Key

	1 P	2 A	W			3 R			4 K	O	5 R	S	H	A	K		
		6 A	R	N	O	L	D				A					7 M	
		G				H			8 P	E	N	N	Y			I	
		O				M			U		D					C	
9 K	I	10 N	D	N	E	S	S	11 S		Z		Y				H	
N		I				R		12 I	Z	Z	Y		13 C		A		
A		A						X		L		14 D	R	A	P	E	R
P		M		15 L	E	T	T	E	R			R				L	
P		O				H						R				16 T	
		17 N	O	A	H			18 G	19 E	R	S	H	O	M		R	
		D							T			L				E	
		20 S	I	N	G	H		21 H		22 O	23 L	U	C	A	S	
	24 V	E	T			A		A		P				T			
		E				25 M	O	N	K	E	Y			S			
		I								R							
		26 G	I	N	G	E	R		27 P	A	R	A	P	L	E	G	I C

Across

1. Kind of prints on the wedding invitations
4. Bus driver for Epiphany
6. Ginger's understudy
8. Julian magically placed one in the hand of each of The Souls.
9. The Souls found this on their journey.
12. Margaret's husband; Nadia's grandfather
14. Margaret's last name before marrying Izzy
15. B & B: a kind of ____ Noah had to write
17. Best man at the wedding
18. Dr. __: Noah's father; Nadia's mother works for him
20. Julian's last name
23. Ethan's older, perfect brother
24. Ham's mother's occupation
25. Julian's toy symbolizing balance: ivory ___
26. Nadia's dog
27. Word describing Mrs. Olinski's physical condition

Down

2. Noah used his red one to transport things to the clubhouse.
3. District Superintendent of Clarion County
5. Ginger's stage role
7. Arnold's owner
8. Gift Ethan takes to the first tea party
9. Ham's last name
10. Izzy's last name
11. Grade level of the Academic Bowl team students
13. Author of Alice in Wonderland
16. Ham laced Ginger's with tranquilizers and laxatives
19. Margaret's grandson
21. He takes Julian's book bag.
22. Ethan really enjoyed this performance: Phantom of the ___

The View From Saturday Crossword 3

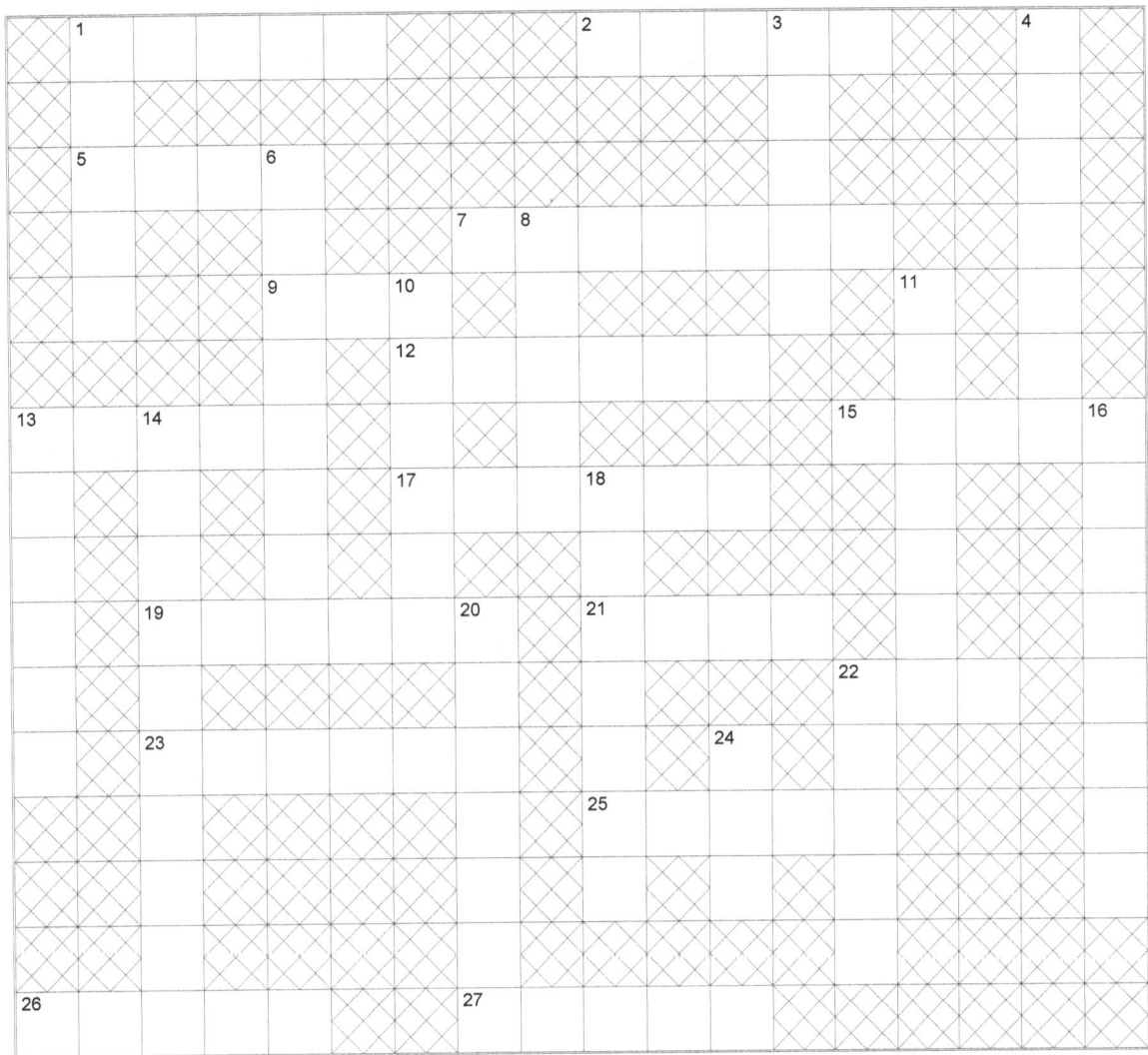

Across
1. Grade level of the Academic Bowl team students
2. Noah used his red one to transport things to the clubhouse.
5. Best man at the wedding
7. Village where Margaret and Izzy live
9. Ham's mother's occupation
12. District Superintendent of Clarion County
13. Nadia had the longest strip of wall ___.
15. Name of the Academic Bowl team: The ___
17. Ginger's understudy
19. Nadia spends this month with her father.
21. Margaret's husband; Nadia's grandfather
22. Kind of prints on the wedding invitations
23. B & B: a kind of ____ Noah had to write
25. Ham's last name
26. Ethan's older, perfect brother
27. Ginger's stage role

Down
1. Julian's last name
3. Ethan really enjoyed this performance: Phantom of the ___
4. Arnold's owner
6. Nadia's father's new best thing
8. Margaret's grandson
10. Ham laced Ginger's with tranquilizers and laxatives
11. State where Nadia's father lives
13. Gift Ethan takes to the first tea party
14. Word describing Mrs. Olinski's physical condition
16. Portion of the North Atlantic where marine life thrives: ___ Sea
18. She selects the Academic Bowl team members.
20. They brought Margaret and Izzy together.
22. Nadia takes this gift to the first tea party
24. He takes Julian's book bag.

The View From Saturday Crossword 3 Answer Key

Across
1. Grade level of the Academic Bowl team students
2. Noah used his red one to transport things to the clubhouse.
5. Best man at the wedding
7. Village where Margaret and Izzy live
9. Ham's mother's occupation
12. District Superintendent of Clarion County
13. Nadia had the longest strip of wall ___.
15. Name of the Academic Bowl team: The ___
17. Ginger's understudy
19. Nadia spends this month with her father.
21. Margaret's husband; Nadia's grandfather
22. Kind of prints on the wedding invitations
23. B & B: a kind of ____ Noah had to write
25. Ham's last name
26. Ethan's older, perfect brother
27. Ginger's stage role

Down
1. Julian's last name
3. Ethan really enjoyed this performance: Phantom of the ___
4. Arnold's owner
6. Nadia's father's new best thing
8. Margaret's grandson
10. Ham laced Ginger's with tranquilizers and laxatives
11. State where Nadia's father lives
13. Gift Ethan takes to the first tea party
14. Word describing Mrs. Olinski's physical condition
16. Portion of the North Atlantic where marine life thrives: ___ Sea
18. She selects the Academic Bowl team members.
20. They brought Margaret and Izzy together.
22. Nadia takes this gift to the first tea party
24. He takes Julian's book bag.

42
Copyrighted

The View From Saturday Crossword 4

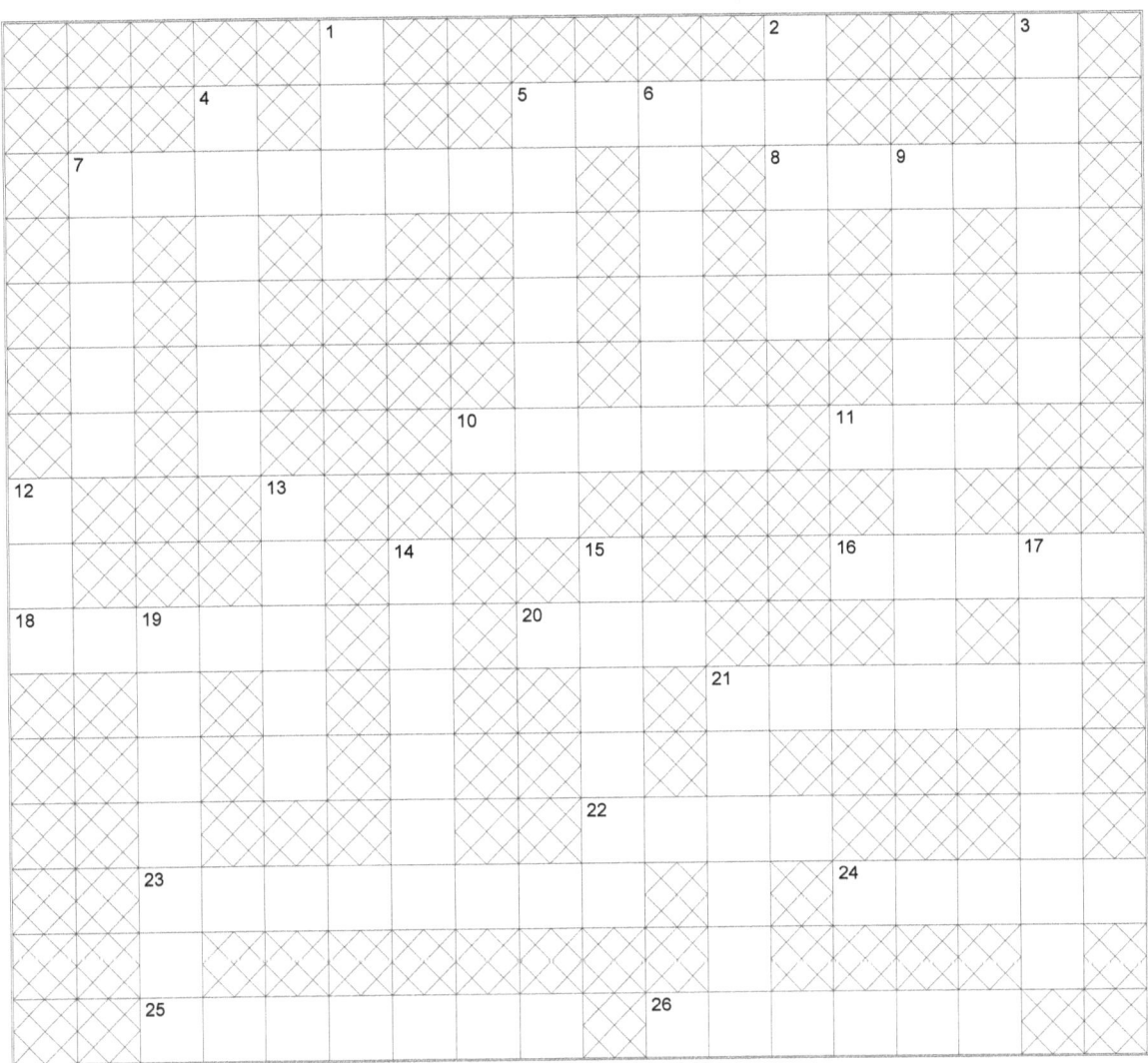

Across
5. Ham's last name
7. Portion of the North Atlantic where marine life thrives: ___ Sea
8. Margaret's grandson
10. Ginger's stage role
11. Ham's mother's occupation
16. Grade level of the Academic Bowl team students
18. Noah used his red one to transport things to the clubhouse.
20. He takes Julian's book bag.
21. Ethan or Lucas
22. Margaret's husband; Nadia's grandfather
23. Nadia's father's new best thing
24. Nadia had the longest strip of wall ___.
25. Arnold's owner
26. B & B: a kind of ____ Noah had to write

Down
1. Best man at the wedding
2. Ethan really enjoyed this performance: Phantom of the ___
3. Nadia's dog
4. Ham laced Ginger's with tranquilizers and laxatives
5. Bus driver for Epiphany
6. Ginger's understudy
7. Julian's last name
9. Nadia's mother is a dental ___.
12. Kind of prints on the wedding invitations
13. Julian magically placed one in the hand of each of The Souls.
14. District Superintendent of Clarion County
15. Term meaning pleasingly plump
17. They brought Margaret and Izzy together.
19. Dr. __: Noah's father; Nadia's mother works for him
21. Gift Ethan takes to the first tea party

The View From Saturday Crossword 4 Answer Key

Across
- 5. Ham's last name
- 7. Portion of the North Atlantic where marine life thrives: ___ Sea
- 8. Margaret's grandson
- 10. Ginger's stage role
- 11. Ham's mother's occupation
- 16. Grade level of the Academic Bowl team students
- 18. Noah used his red one to transport things to the clubhouse.
- 20. He takes Julian's book bag.
- 21. Ethan or Lucas
- 22. Margaret's husband; Nadia's grandfather
- 23. Nadia's father's new best thing
- 24. Nadia had the longest strip of wall ___.
- 25. Arnold's owner
- 26. B & B: a kind of ____ Noah had to write

Down
- 1. Best man at the wedding
- 2. Ethan really enjoyed this performance: Phantom of the ___
- 3. Nadia's dog
- 4. Ham laced Ginger's with tranquilizers and laxatives
- 5. Bus driver for Epiphany
- 6. Ginger's understudy
- 7. Julian's last name
- 9. Nadia's mother is a dental ___.
- 12. Kind of prints on the wedding invitations
- 13. Julian magically placed one in the hand of each of The Souls.
- 14. District Superintendent of Clarion County
- 15. Term meaning pleasingly plump
- 17. They brought Margaret and Izzy together.
- 19. Dr. __: Noah's father; Nadia's mother works for him
- 21. Gift Ethan takes to the first tea party

Filled grid answers:
- 5A. KNAPP
- 7A. SARGASSO
- 8A. ETHAN
- 10A. SANDY
- 11A. VET
- 16A. SIXTH
- 18A. WAGON
- 20A. HAM
- 21A. POTTER
- 22A. IZZY
- 23A. HOVERING
- 24A. PAPER
- 25A. MICHAEL
- 26A. LETTER
- 1D. NOTHING
- 2D. OPERA
- 3D. GINGER
- 4D. TEAHEATS (T-E-A-H-S... actually: TEATS? — shown: T,E,A,H,S along column for 4D)
- 5D. KNORSHLY (K,N,R,S,H,L — column letters)
- 6D. APRONAG (A,P,R,O,A — column letters)
- 7D. SINGH
- 8D. EYGI
- 9D. HYGIENIST
- 12D. PAW
- 13D. PENNYS
- 14D. ROHMME
- 15D. ZAFTIG
- 17D. TUTRTL (T,U,R,T,L)
- 19D. GERSHOM (G,E,R,S)
- 21D. PUZZL

The View From Saturday

SARGASSO	VET	ZATFIG	PENNY	MICHAEL
ROHMER	PUZZLE	PAW	CALLIGRAPHY	HAM
OLINSKI	EPIPHANY	FREE SPACE	PARAPLEGIC	TURTLES
DIAMONDSTEIN	LUCAS	KNAPP	HOVERING	SOULS
SANDY	SINGH	HYGIENIST	SIXTH	SILLINGTON

The View From Saturday

NOAH	MARGARET	WAGON	AUGUST	KORSHAK
GINGER	CARROLL	LETTER	MAXWELL	KINDNESS
ETHAN	PUPPY	FREE SPACE	MONKEY	PAPER
ARNOLD	TREATS	FAIRBAIN	POTTER	DRAPER
GERSHOM	FLORIDA	CENTURY	SILLINGTON	SIXTH

The View From Saturday

SOULS	FLORIDA	PUZZLE	KNAPP	MARGARET
TURTLES	AUGUST	SANDY	ROHMER	SINGH
OPERA	TREATS	FREE SPACE	VET	CALLIGRAPHY
SARGASSO	CENTURY	HAM	KINDNESS	GINGER
MONKEY	MAXWELL	HOVERING	LETTER	MICHAEL

The View From Saturday

PAW	SIXTH	DIAMONDSTEIN	PAPER	LUCAS
ARNOLD	WAGON	NOAH	OLINSKI	ZATFIG
DRAPER	CARROLL	FREE SPACE	PARAPLEGIC	SILLINGTON
FAIRBAIN	KORSHAK	EPIPHANY	PUPPY	ETHAN
PENNY	HYGIENIST	POTTER	MICHAEL	LETTER

The View From Saturday

KORSHAK	FAIRBAIN	ETHAN	SIXTH	TREATS
PENNY	FLORIDA	PUZZLE	CENTURY	KNAPP
CALLIGRAPHY	SARGASSO	FREE SPACE	GINGER	SILLINGTON
HOVERING	PUPPY	ZATFIG	KINDNESS	CARROLL
OPERA	MARGARET	HYGIENIST	NOAH	ROHMER

The View From Saturday

IZZY	HAM	LUCAS	DIAMONDSTEIN	VET
SOULS	SANDY	PAPER	OLINSKI	POTTER
TURTLES	MICHAEL	FREE SPACE	MONKEY	LETTER
PARAPLEGIC	AUGUST	PAW	SINGH	GERSHOM
MAXWELL	EPIPHANY	WAGON	ROHMER	NOAH

The View From Saturday

KNAPP	MARGARET	LUCAS	HYGIENIST	KORSHAK
CARROLL	OLINSKI	GERSHOM	CALLIGRAPHY	SIXTH
DRAPER	PAPER	FREE SPACE	CENTURY	SARGASSO
HAM	ROHMER	ARNOLD	FLORIDA	NOAH
WAGON	GINGER	DIAMONDSTEIN	ETHAN	VET

The View From Saturday

PENNY	PAW	MICHAEL	KINDNESS	SANDY
TREATS	LETTER	SILLINGTON	SINGH	PARAPLEGIC
OPERA	SOULS	FREE SPACE	FAIRBAIN	IZZY
PUZZLE	POTTER	TURTLES	MAXWELL	AUGUST
ZATFIG	PUPPY	MONKEY	VET	ETHAN

The View From Saturday

SINGH	IZZY	EPIPHANY	ROHMER	PAPER
DIAMONDSTEIN	ARNOLD	HAM	SILLINGTON	NOAH
KINDNESS	PUPPY	FREE SPACE	LETTER	DRAPER
FLORIDA	OLINSKI	MARGARET	CALLIGRAPHY	VET
TURTLES	LUCAS	SOULS	HOVERING	CENTURY

The View From Saturday

PARAPLEGIC	CARROLL	KNAPP	ZATFIG	MAXWELL
SARGASSO	WAGON	ETHAN	SIXTH	OPERA
FAIRBAIN	PUZZLE	FREE SPACE	PAW	MONKEY
TREATS	AUGUST	SANDY	HYGIENIST	GERSHOM
PENNY	MICHAEL	KORSHAK	CENTURY	HOVERING

The View From Saturday

MAXWELL	PENNY	SOULS	PAPER	SARGASSO
KNAPP	CALLIGRAPHY	PARAPLEGIC	HYGIENIST	SILLINGTON
TURTLES	SINGH	FREE SPACE	HAM	EPIPHANY
ARNOLD	CENTURY	OPERA	IZZY	DIAMONDSTEIN
LUCAS	MARGARET	PUPPY	LETTER	MICHAEL

The View From Saturday

NOAH	MONKEY	SANDY	VET	SIXTH
AUGUST	GERSHOM	KORSHAK	TREATS	CARROLL
PAW	DRAPER	FREE SPACE	ZATFIG	FAIRBAIN
ETHAN	WAGON	HOVERING	GINGER	ROHMER
POTTER	PUZZLE	OLINSKI	MICHAEL	LETTER

The View From Saturday

TREATS	MONKEY	PARAPLEGIC	KORSHAK	POTTER
ARNOLD	GINGER	SILLINGTON	LUCAS	PAW
FAIRBAIN	ETHAN	FREE SPACE	SARGASSO	FLORIDA
IZZY	DRAPER	PUPPY	MAXWELL	SINGH
PAPER	CARROLL	MARGARET	TURTLES	PENNY

The View From Saturday

LETTER	PUZZLE	ROHMER	ZATFIG	OLINSKI
SIXTH	MICHAEL	SOULS	HYGIENIST	VET
HOVERING	EPIPHANY	FREE SPACE	OPERA	GERSHOM
HAM	DIAMONDSTEIN	KINDNESS	SANDY	AUGUST
NOAH	WAGON	KNAPP	PENNY	TURTLES

The View From Saturday

LUCAS	MICHAEL	PUZZLE	TREATS	HOVERING
ROHMER	OPERA	LETTER	MONKEY	CALLIGRAPHY
CENTURY	MARGARET	FREE SPACE	KNAPP	IZZY
AUGUST	ETHAN	ZATFIG	FLORIDA	SOULS
SANDY	HYGIENIST	DRAPER	GERSHOM	GINGER

The View From Saturday

ARNOLD	PENNY	TURTLES	KINDNESS	OLINSKI
PARAPLEGIC	SIXTH	PUPPY	SARGASSO	POTTER
HAM	SINGH	FREE SPACE	KORSHAK	CARROLL
PAW	NOAH	WAGON	MAXWELL	VET
EPIPHANY	DIAMONDSTEIN	PAPER	GINGER	GERSHOM

The View From Saturday

FAIRBAIN	DIAMONDSTEIN	SIXTH	TREATS	KORSHAK
OLINSKI	CARROLL	SARGASSO	TURTLES	SANDY
PARAPLEGIC	PAW	FREE SPACE	ETHAN	PUPPY
ARNOLD	LETTER	MICHAEL	HOVERING	FLORIDA
CALLIGRAPHY	KNAPP	LUCAS	MONKEY	OPERA

The View From Saturday

AUGUST	SOULS	MARGARET	IZZY	PUZZLE
CENTURY	KINDNESS	EPIPHANY	ROHMER	GINGER
VET	ZATFIG	FREE SPACE	SINGH	WAGON
HYGIENIST	DRAPER	POTTER	MAXWELL	HAM
PENNY	SILLINGTON	PAPER	OPERA	MONKEY

The View From Saturday

KINDNESS	NOAH	CENTURY	KORSHAK	PENNY
HAM	MICHAEL	PUZZLE	KNAPP	DIAMONDSTEIN
SOULS	WAGON	FREE SPACE	FAIRBAIN	PAPER
ZATFIG	PARAPLEGIC	MARGARET	SIXTH	SANDY
GINGER	ARNOLD	OPERA	SINGH	EPIPHANY

The View From Saturday

DRAPER	CALLIGRAPHY	HOVERING	MONKEY	ROHMER
VET	SARGASSO	PAW	ETHAN	POTTER
IZZY	HYGIENIST	FREE SPACE	OLINSKI	AUGUST
LETTER	FLORIDA	TURTLES	MAXWELL	CARROLL
TREATS	GERSHOM	PUPPY	EPIPHANY	SINGH

The View From Saturday

TURTLES	ARNOLD	SILLINGTON	ZATFIG	HOVERING
PARAPLEGIC	LUCAS	VET	TREATS	CALLIGRAPHY
PUZZLE	DRAPER	FREE SPACE	MICHAEL	POTTER
GERSHOM	HYGIENIST	PAW	SIXTH	SARGASSO
MARGARET	SINGH	AUGUST	PAPER	CENTURY

The View From Saturday

FAIRBAIN	SANDY	LETTER	WAGON	KINDNESS
EPIPHANY	DIAMONDSTEIN	OPERA	FLORIDA	MAXWELL
KORSHAK	NOAH	FREE SPACE	PUPPY	ETHAN
GINGER	PENNY	KNAPP	CARROLL	ROHMER
MONKEY	IZZY	HAM	CENTURY	PAPER

The View From Saturday

ETHAN	PUZZLE	PAPER	HYGIENIST	PARAPLEGIC
ARNOLD	KINDNESS	HOVERING	KORSHAK	AUGUST
WAGON	MICHAEL	FREE SPACE	MONKEY	SANDY
DIAMONDSTEIN	EPIPHANY	IZZY	FLORIDA	SIXTH
DRAPER	MARGARET	SOULS	LUCAS	POTTER

The View From Saturday

GERSHOM	SILLINGTON	MAXWELL	ROHMER	HAM
OLINSKI	PUPPY	CENTURY	VET	LETTER
PAW	GINGER	FREE SPACE	CALLIGRAPHY	TREATS
KNAPP	ZATFIG	FAIRBAIN	TURTLES	OPERA
SINGH	NOAH	PENNY	POTTER	LUCAS

The View From Saturday

EPIPHANY	VET	DIAMONDSTEIN	IZZY	TURTLES
PUPPY	MAXWELL	ROHMER	SOULS	ETHAN
FAIRBAIN	LUCAS	FREE SPACE	OPERA	SILLINGTON
ARNOLD	NOAH	MONKEY	LETTER	AUGUST
HYGIENIST	FLORIDA	GERSHOM	KORSHAK	KNAPP

The View From Saturday

CALLIGRAPHY	CARROLL	WAGON	SIXTH	CENTURY
HAM	PARAPLEGIC	MARGARET	SARGASSO	GINGER
POTTER	TREATS	FREE SPACE	PUZZLE	SANDY
MICHAEL	HOVERING	PENNY	ZATFIG	OLINSKI
KINDNESS	DRAPER	PAW	KNAPP	KORSHAK

The View From Saturday

DIAMONDSTEIN	SIXTH	GERSHOM	ETHAN	CARROLL
KINDNESS	PAPER	HAM	SANDY	KNAPP
VET	KORSHAK	FREE SPACE	WAGON	FAIRBAIN
HOVERING	GINGER	MARGARET	LETTER	MICHAEL
SARGASSO	IZZY	PUPPY	EPIPHANY	PARAPLEGIC

The View From Saturday

AUGUST	SINGH	PENNY	TREATS	OLINSKI
ARNOLD	ROHMER	PUZZLE	NOAH	TURTLES
PAW	DRAPER	FREE SPACE	CENTURY	MONKEY
ZATFIG	SILLINGTON	LUCAS	OPERA	SOULS
HYGIENIST	FLORIDA	MAXWELL	PARAPLEGIC	EPIPHANY

The View From Saturday

PUZZLE	DRAPER	ROHMER	OLINSKI	HAM
IZZY	FLORIDA	SOULS	WAGON	TURTLES
NOAH	HYGIENIST	FREE SPACE	SANDY	MAXWELL
PENNY	SILLINGTON	ARNOLD	POTTER	CARROLL
SIXTH	SARGASSO	MICHAEL	VET	PUPPY

The View From Saturday

KNAPP	LUCAS	FAIRBAIN	PARAPLEGIC	LETTER
MARGARET	CENTURY	TREATS	GERSHOM	OPERA
EPIPHANY	CALLIGRAPHY	FREE SPACE	PAPER	GINGER
SINGH	KINDNESS	KORSHAK	ETHAN	DIAMONDSTEIN
HOVERING	ZATFIG	PAW	PUPPY	VET

The View From Saturday

OPERA	LUCAS	KINDNESS	FLORIDA	SINGH
SILLINGTON	HAM	GERSHOM	MARGARET	CENTURY
DRAPER	PUPPY	FREE SPACE	OLINSKI	PENNY
WAGON	HYGIENIST	SARGASSO	NOAH	CALLIGRAPHY
AUGUST	PAW	POTTER	ETHAN	PARAPLEGIC

The View From Saturday

HOVERING	PAPER	MICHAEL	GINGER	CARROLL
TURTLES	TREATS	KORSHAK	SOULS	SANDY
MAXWELL	ZATFIG	FREE SPACE	KNAPP	PUZZLE
VET	FAIRBAIN	SIXTH	ROHMER	IZZY
ARNOLD	DIAMONDSTEIN	EPIPHANY	PARAPLEGIC	ETHAN

View From Saturday Vocabulary Word List

No.	Word	Clue/Definition
1.	ACCURATE	Precisely correct
2.	ACQUIRE	To learn or possess
3.	ACRONYMS	Word created from the initial letters of words in a longer phrase
4.	ADMONISH	Warn
5.	ADORN	Decorate splendidly
6.	ADVISED	Offered advice; recommended
7.	AMBLED	Strolled or walked leisurely
8.	ANIMATED	Lively
9.	APPOINT	Assign people to a certain task or job
10.	ARCHIVE	Collection of historical documents or records
11.	ATROCIOUSLY	Extremely badly
12.	BATED	Tapered off; became smaller or less
13.	BENEVOLENTLY	Kindly
14.	BRAWN	Physical strength
15.	CAPSULE	Compact and succinct
16.	CARAFE	Glass receptacle with an open top used for holding liquid
17.	CARDINAL	Fundamental
18.	COIFFED	Characterized by carefully styled, immaculate hairdo
19.	COMPLEMENTARY	Combining in such a way as to enhance each other
20.	CONCLUDED	Decided through reasoning and deliberation
21.	CONVERGED	Came from different directions toward a central point
22.	CONVERSION	Something that has changed into another form, substance, state, or product
23.	DECORUM	Etiquette; proper social behavior
24.	DEFACTO	Existing in fact
25.	DEFINITELY	Without doubt
26.	DICTATORIAL	Behaving as if one has complete rule over others
27.	DISENTANGLED	Untwisted
28.	DIVERSITY	Variety
29.	DOMICILES	Homes
30.	ECOLOGY	Branch of biology examining the relationship of organisms to one another and their environment
31.	EXCESSIVE	More than is needed or wanted
32.	FAVORABLE	Showing approval
33.	FEEBLE	Weak
34.	FRIEZE	Horizontal band of decoration in a building
35.	GENUS	In biology, a category above species and below family
36.	HOVERED	Lingered without purpose
37.	INCANDESCENTLY	Glowingly
38.	INCUBATING	Keeping eggs warm until hatchlings emerge
39.	INEVITABLE	Certain; with an unavoidable outcome
40.	INVENTORY	List of the quantity of items contained in an area
41.	INVOLUNTARILY	Doing something against one's will
42.	IRONIC	Occurring in a manner opposite to what is expected
43.	ITINERANT	Traveling
44.	JUBILANT	Triumphantly happy
45.	KNOLL	Small hill
46.	LECTERN	Podium
47.	MAIMED	Injured permanently
48.	MALICE	Wanting to do harm
49.	MAMMOTH	Huge

View From Saturday Vocabulary Word List

No.	Word	Clue/Definition
50.	MECHANISM	Method or instinct an animal has for finding its way
51.	MEDIOCRE	Average to below average in quality
52.	MULTICULTURALISM	Pertaining to a variety of cultural groups
53.	NANOSECOND	Tiniest fraction of a second
54.	NATURALIZATION	Process of granting citizenship to a foreigner
55.	NEGLECT	Inattention
56.	NONCHALANTLY	In a relaxed manner
57.	ORIGINATE	Have a beginning
58.	PARCELED	Divided into smaller units
59.	PERPETUAL	Continuing without change or end
60.	PHALANX	Unit of troops who stand closely together
61.	PRECEDED	To have gone before
62.	PRECEDENT	Previous event that serves as an example in the future
63.	PRECISION	Exact in detail
64.	PREOCCUPIED	Consumed by the thought of something
65.	PRETEXT	False excuse
66.	PROTRUDING	Sticking out
67.	QUAINT	Charmingly old-fashioned
68.	QUARTERING	Able to cut into fourths
69.	REFRAINED	Kept oneself from doing something
70.	REINFORCE	Strengthen
71.	RENDERING	Version or translation
72.	REVISED	Reconsidered; altered; amended; improved
73.	RUCKUS	Commotion
74.	SENTINELS	Guards
75.	SOPHISTICATED	Having worldly experience or culture
76.	SOVEREIGN	King who is supreme ruler
77.	SPONTANEOUS	Occurring without planning or warning
78.	STRICT	Without relaxation or distraction
79.	SUPPRESSED	Prevented from being expressed; kept down
80.	SYLLABICATION	Having to do with the parts of words
81.	TERMINALLY	Irreversibly
82.	TORMENT	Intense suffering
83.	TRAJECTORY	Path a flying object takes
84.	TRANQUILIZE	Administer a drug that will soothe or calm
85.	TRANSLUCENCE	State of being semi-transparent
86.	UNFURL	Spread out from a folded position
87.	UNRULY	Hard to control
88.	VERGE	A point or limit
89.	VULGAR	Lacking charm, culture, or sophistication

View From Saturday Vocabulary Fill In The Blanks 1

_____ 1. Occurring in a manner opposite to what is expected

_____ 2. Able to cut into fourths

_____ 3. In biology, a category above species and below family

_____ 4. Strolled or walked leisurely

_____ 5. Existing in fact

_____ 6. Average to below average in quality

_____ 7. Behaving as if one has complete rule over others

_____ 8. Lively

_____ 9. Commotion

_____ 10. Occurring without planning or warning

_____ 11. In a relaxed manner

_____ 12. Decided through reasoning and deliberation

_____ 13. Variety

_____ 14. State of being semi-transparent

_____ 15. Consumed by the thought of something

_____ 16. Showing approval

_____ 17. Divided into smaller units

_____ 18. Doing something against one's will

_____ 19. Unit of troops who stand closely together

_____ 20. Previous event that serves as an example in the future

View From Saturday Vocabulary Fill In The Blanks 1 Answer Key

IRONIC	1. Occurring in a manner opposite to what is expected
QUARTERING	2. Able to cut into fourths
GENUS	3. In biology, a category above species and below family
AMBLED	4. Strolled or walked leisurely
DEFACTO	5. Existing in fact
MEDIOCRE	6. Average to below average in quality
DICTATORIAL	7. Behaving as if one has complete rule over others
ANIMATED	8. Lively
RUCKUS	9. Commotion
SPONTANEOUS	10. Occurring without planning or warning
NONCHALANTLY	11. In a relaxed manner
CONCLUDED	12. Decided through reasoning and deliberation
DIVERSITY	13. Variety
TRANSLUCENCE	14. State of being semi-transparent
PREOCCUPIED	15. Consumed by the thought of something
FAVORABLE	16. Showing approval
PARCELED	17. Divided into smaller units
INVOLUNTARILY	18. Doing something against one's will
PHALANX	19. Unit of troops who stand closely together
PRECEDENT	20. Previous event that serves as an example in the future

View From Saturday Vocabulary Fill In The Blanks 2

_____ 1. Traveling

_____ 2. Without relaxation or distraction

_____ 3. Small hill

_____ 4. Behaving as if one has complete rule over others

_____ 5. False excuse

_____ 6. Decorate splendidly

_____ 7. Combining in such a way as to enhance each other

_____ 8. Having to do with the parts of words

_____ 9. Something that has changed into another form, substance, state, or product

_____ 10. Fundamental

_____ 11. Variety

_____ 12. Intense suffering

_____ 13. Process of granting citizenship to a foreigner

_____ 14. Podium

_____ 15. Prevented from being expressed; kept down

_____ 16. Hard to control

_____ 17. Unit of troops who stand closely together

_____ 18. Etiquette; proper social behavior

_____ 19. Commotion

_____ 20. Wanting to do harm

View From Saturday Vocabulary Fill In The Blanks 2 Answer Key

ITINERANT	1. Traveling
STRICT	2. Without relaxation or distraction
KNOLL	3. Small hill
DICTATORIAL	4. Behaving as if one has complete rule over others
PRETEXT	5. False excuse
ADORN	6. Decorate splendidly
COMPLEMENTARY	7. Combining in such a way as to enhance each other
SYLLABICATION	8. Having to do with the parts of words
CONVERSION	9. Something that has changed into another form, substance, state, or product
CARDINAL	10. Fundamental
DIVERSITY	11. Variety
TORMENT	12. Intense suffering
NATURALIZATION	13. Process of granting citizenship to a foreigner
LECTERN	14. Podium
SUPPRESSED	15. Prevented from being expressed; kept down
UNRULY	16. Hard to control
PHALANX	17. Unit of troops who stand closely together
DECORUM	18. Etiquette; proper social behavior
RUCKUS	19. Commotion
MALICE	20. Wanting to do harm

View From Saturday Vocabulary Fill In The Blanks 3

_____ 1. Spread out from a folded position

_____ 2. Lingered without purpose

_____ 3. Came from different directions toward a central point

_____ 4. Charmingly old-fashioned

_____ 5. Pertaining to a variety of cultural groups

_____ 6. Commotion

_____ 7. Compact and succinct

_____ 8. Occurring without planning or warning

_____ 9. Assign people to a certain task or job

_____ 10. Branch of biology examining the relationship of organisms to one another and their environment

_____ 11. Continuing without change or end

_____ 12. Sticking out

_____ 13. Exact in detail

_____ 14. Horizontal band of decoration in a building

_____ 15. State of being semi-transparent

_____ 16. Weak

_____ 17. Combining in such a way as to enhance each other

_____ 18. To have gone before

_____ 19. List of the quantity of items contained in an area

_____ 20. Tiniest fraction of a second

View From Saturday Vocabulary Fill In The Blanks 3 Answer Key

UNFURL	1. Spread out from a folded position
HOVERED	2. Lingered without purpose
CONVERGED	3. Came from different directions toward a central point
QUAINT	4. Charmingly old-fashioned
MULTICULTURALISM	5. Pertaining to a variety of cultural groups
RUCKUS	6. Commotion
CAPSULE	7. Compact and succinct
SPONTANEOUS	8. Occurring without planning or warning
APPOINT	9. Assign people to a certain task or job
ECOLOGY	10. Branch of biology examining the relationship of organisms to one another and their environment
PERPETUAL	11. Continuing without change or end
PROTRUDING	12. Sticking out
PRECISION	13. Exact in detail
FRIEZE	14. Horizontal band of decoration in a building
TRANSLUCENCE	15. State of being semi-transparent
FEEBLE	16. Weak
COMPLEMENTARY	17. Combining in such a way as to enhance each other
PRECEDED	18. To have gone before
INVENTORY	19. List of the quantity of items contained in an area
NANOSECOND	20. Tiniest fraction of a second

View From Saturday Vocabulary Fill In The Blanks 4

_____ 1. Triumphantly happy

_____ 2. More than is needed or wanted

_____ 3. Continuing without change or end

_____ 4. Wanting to do harm

_____ 5. Compact and succinct

_____ 6. Weak

_____ 7. Variety

_____ 8. Small hill

_____ 9. Having worldly experience or culture

_____ 10. Having to do with the parts of words

_____ 11. Administer a drug that will soothe or calm

_____ 12. In a relaxed manner

_____ 13. Behaving as if one has complete rule over others

_____ 14. Previous event that serves as an example in the future

_____ 15. False excuse

_____ 16. Decorate splendidly

_____ 17. Reconsidered; altered; amended; improved

_____ 18. Have a beginning

_____ 19. Combining in such a way as to enhance each other

_____ 20. To have gone before

View From Saturday Vocabulary Fill In The Blanks 4 Answer Key

JUBILANT	1. Triumphantly happy
EXCESSIVE	2. More than is needed or wanted
PERPETUAL	3. Continuing without change or end
MALICE	4. Wanting to do harm
CAPSULE	5. Compact and succinct
FEEBLE	6. Weak
DIVERSITY	7. Variety
KNOLL	8. Small hill
SOPHISTICATED	9. Having worldly experience or culture
SYLLABICATION	10. Having to do with the parts of words
TRANQUILIZE	11. Administer a drug that will soothe or calm
NONCHALANTLY	12. In a relaxed manner
DICTATORIAL	13. Behaving as if one has complete rule over others
PRECEDENT	14. Previous event that serves as an example in the future
PRETEXT	15. False excuse
ADORN	16. Decorate splendidly
REVISED	17. Reconsidered; altered; amended; improved
ORIGINATE	18. Have a beginning
COMPLEMENTARY	19. Combining in such a way as to enhance each other
PRECEDED	20. To have gone before

View From Saturday Vocabulary Matching 1

___ 1. TORMENT
___ 2. SOVEREIGN
___ 3. ORIGINATE
___ 4. DISENTANGLED
___ 5. SUPPRESSED
___ 6. STRICT
___ 7. UNFURL
___ 8. PRETEXT
___ 9. DEFACTO
___ 10. COMPLEMENTARY
___ 11. PRECEDED
___ 12. VERGE
___ 13. LECTERN
___ 14. PERPETUAL
___ 15. ADMONISH
___ 16. RENDERING
___ 17. PROTRUDING
___ 18. REINFORCE
___ 19. INEVITABLE
___ 20. APPOINT
___ 21. ADVISED
___ 22. EXCESSIVE
___ 23. NATURALIZATION
___ 24. DEFINITELY
___ 25. BRAWN

A. To have gone before
B. Without doubt
C. Process of granting citizenship to a foreigner
D. A point or limit
E. False excuse
F. Intense suffering
G. Warn
H. Combining in such a way as to enhance each other
I. Untwisted
J. Assign people to a certain task or job
K. Existing in fact
L. Continuing without change or end
M. More than is needed or wanted
N. Version or translation
O. Podium
P. Without relaxation or distraction
Q. Certain; with an unavoidable outcome
R. Have a beginning
S. Offered advice; recommended
T. Strengthen
U. Physical strength
V. Sticking out
W. King who is supreme ruler
X. Prevented from being expressed; kept down
Y. Spread out from a folded position

View From Saturday Vocabulary Matching 1 Answer Key

F - 1.	TORMENT	A. To have gone before
W - 2.	SOVEREIGN	B. Without doubt
R - 3.	ORIGINATE	C. Process of granting citizenship to a foreigner
I - 4.	DISENTANGLED	D. A point or limit
X - 5.	SUPPRESSED	E. False excuse
P - 6.	STRICT	F. Intense suffering
Y - 7.	UNFURL	G. Warn
E - 8.	PRETEXT	H. Combining in such a way as to enhance each other
K - 9.	DEFACTO	I. Untwisted
H - 10.	COMPLEMENTARY	J. Assign people to a certain task or job
A - 11.	PRECEDED	K. Existing in fact
D - 12.	VERGE	L. Continuing without change or end
O - 13.	LECTERN	M. More than is needed or wanted
L - 14.	PERPETUAL	N. Version or translation
G - 15.	ADMONISH	O. Podium
N - 16.	RENDERING	P. Without relaxation or distraction
V - 17.	PROTRUDING	Q. Certain; with an unavoidable outcome
T - 18.	REINFORCE	R. Have a beginning
Q - 19.	INEVITABLE	S. Offered advice; recommended
J - 20.	APPOINT	T. Strengthen
S - 21.	ADVISED	U. Physical strength
M - 22.	EXCESSIVE	V. Sticking out
C - 23.	NATURALIZATION	W. King who is supreme ruler
B - 24.	DEFINITELY	X. Prevented from being expressed; kept down
U - 25.	BRAWN	Y. Spread out from a folded position

View From Saturday Vocabulary Matching 2

___ 1. FRIEZE
___ 2. PRECEDED
___ 3. FAVORABLE
___ 4. INVENTORY
___ 5. BRAWN
___ 6. PRETEXT
___ 7. COIFFED
___ 8. QUAINT
___ 9. IRONIC
___ 10. JUBILANT
___ 11. DICTATORIAL
___ 12. SYLLABICATION
___ 13. SENTINELS
___ 14. PRECEDENT
___ 15. GENUS
___ 16. CARDINAL
___ 17. ACQUIRE
___ 18. DEFINITELY
___ 19. REINFORCE
___ 20. CONCLUDED
___ 21. PREOCCUPIED
___ 22. LECTERN
___ 23. NONCHALANTLY
___ 24. DOMICILES
___ 25. TERMINALLY

A. Without doubt
B. Having to do with the parts of words
C. Strengthen
D. Podium
E. Horizontal band of decoration in a building
F. Decided through reasoning and deliberation
G. Behaving as if one has complete rule over others
H. To have gone before
I. Characterized by carefully styled, immaculate hairdo
J. List of the quantity of items contained in an area
K. In a relaxed manner
L. Showing approval
M. Triumphantly happy
N. Irreversibly
O. Occurring in a manner opposite to what is expected
P. Guards
Q. False excuse
R. Consumed by the thought of something
S. Charmingly old-fashioned
T. Previous event that serves as an example in the future
U. To learn or possess
V. In biology, a category above species and below family
W. Physical strength
X. Fundamental
Y. Homes

View From Saturday Vocabulary Matching 2 Answer Key

E - 1. FRIEZE
H - 2. PRECEDED
L - 3. FAVORABLE
J - 4. INVENTORY
W - 5. BRAWN
Q - 6. PRETEXT
I - 7. COIFFED
S - 8. QUAINT
O - 9. IRONIC
M - 10. JUBILANT
G - 11. DICTATORIAL
B - 12. SYLLABICATION
P - 13. SENTINELS
T - 14. PRECEDENT
V - 15. GENUS
X - 16. CARDINAL
U - 17. ACQUIRE
A - 18. DEFINITELY
C - 19. REINFORCE
F - 20. CONCLUDED
R - 21. PREOCCUPIED
D - 22. LECTERN
K - 23. NONCHALANTLY
Y - 24. DOMICILES
N - 25. TERMINALLY

A. Without doubt
B. Having to do with the parts of words
C. Strengthen
D. Podium
E. Horizontal band of decoration in a building
F. Decided through reasoning and deliberation
G. Behaving as if one has complete rule over others
H. To have gone before
I. Characterized by carefully styled, immaculate hairdo
J. List of the quantity of items contained in an area
K. In a relaxed manner
L. Showing approval
M. Triumphantly happy
N. Irreversibly
O. Occurring in a manner opposite to what is expected
P. Guards
Q. False excuse
R. Consumed by the thought of something
S. Charmingly old-fashioned
T. Previous event that serves as an example in the future
U. To learn or possess
V. In biology, a category above species and below family
W. Physical strength
X. Fundamental
Y. Homes

View From Saturday Vocabulary Matching 3

___ 1. CAPSULE
___ 2. APPOINT
___ 3. SPONTANEOUS
___ 4. LECTERN
___ 5. ADORN
___ 6. FRIEZE
___ 7. PROTRUDING
___ 8. JUBILANT
___ 9. DOMICILES
___ 10. CONCLUDED
___ 11. ECOLOGY
___ 12. RENDERING
___ 13. RUCKUS
___ 14. NATURALIZATION
___ 15. MAMMOTH
___ 16. FEEBLE
___ 17. NANOSECOND
___ 18. TRANQUILIZE
___ 19. MEDIOCRE
___ 20. MAIMED
___ 21. QUAINT
___ 22. ACCURATE
___ 23. PRETEXT
___ 24. TERMINALLY
___ 25. BATED

A. Occurring without planning or warning
B. Precisely correct
C. Version or translation
D. Weak
E. Irreversibly
F. Decorate splendidly
G. Injured permanently
H. Horizontal band of decoration in a building
I. Tiniest fraction of a second
J. Charmingly old-fashioned
K. Administer a drug that will soothe or calm
L. Podium
M. Process of granting citizenship to a foreigner
N. Sticking out
O. Assign people to a certain task or job
P. Branch of biology examining the relationship of organisms to one another and their environment
Q. False excuse
R. Tapered off; became smaller or less
S. Average to below average in quality
T. Commotion
U. Decided through reasoning and deliberation
V. Compact and succinct
W. Triumphantly happy
X. Huge
Y. Homes

View From Saturday Vocabulary Matching 3 Answer Key

V - 1. CAPSULE
O - 2. APPOINT
A - 3. SPONTANEOUS
L - 4. LECTERN
F - 5. ADORN
H - 6. FRIEZE
N - 7. PROTRUDING
W - 8. JUBILANT
Y - 9. DOMICILES
U - 10. CONCLUDED
P - 11. ECOLOGY
C - 12. RENDERING
T - 13. RUCKUS
M - 14. NATURALIZATION
X - 15. MAMMOTH
D - 16. FEEBLE
I - 17. NANOSECOND
K - 18. TRANQUILIZE
S - 19. MEDIOCRE
G - 20. MAIMED
J - 21. QUAINT
B - 22. ACCURATE
Q - 23. PRETEXT
E - 24. TERMINALLY
R - 25. BATED

A. Occurring without planning or warning
B. Precisely correct
C. Version or translation
D. Weak
E. Irreversibly
F. Decorate splendidly
G. Injured permanently
H. Horizontal band of decoration in a building
I. Tiniest fraction of a second
J. Charmingly old-fashioned
K. Administer a drug that will soothe or calm
L. Podium
M. Process of granting citizenship to a foreigner
N. Sticking out
O. Assign people to a certain task or job
P. Branch of biology examining the relationship of organisms to one another and their environment
Q. False excuse
R. Tapered off; became smaller or less
S. Average to below average in quality
T. Commotion
U. Decided through reasoning and deliberation
V. Compact and succinct
W. Triumphantly happy
X. Huge
Y. Homes

View From Saturday Vocabulary Matching 4

___ 1. NEGLECT   A. Tiniest fraction of a second
___ 2. RENDERING   B. State of being semi-transparent
___ 3. BRAWN   C. Decorate splendidly
___ 4. TRANSLUCENCE   D. Version or translation
___ 5. REVISED   E. Lingered without purpose
___ 6. INEVITABLE   F. Injured permanently
___ 7. TRAJECTORY   G. Small hill
___ 8. PERPETUAL   H. Reconsidered; altered; amended; improved
___ 9. PROTRUDING   I. List of the quantity of items contained in an area
___10. DISENTANGLED   J. Divided into smaller units
___11. KNOLL   K. Continuing without change or end
___12. INVENTORY   L. Certain; with an unavoidable outcome
___13. UNFURL   M. A point or limit
___14. COIFFED   N. Path a flying object takes
___15. PARCELED   O. Able to cut into fourths
___16. ADMONISH   P. Sticking out
___17. ANIMATED   Q. Physical strength
___18. HOVERED   R. Characterized by carefully styled, immaculate hairdo
___19. VERGE   S. Spread out from a folded position
___20. ADORN   T. Traveling
___21. QUARTERING   U. Warn
___22. ITINERANT   V. Lively
___23. CONVERSION   W. Untwisted
___24. NANOSECOND   X. Something that has changed into another form, substance, state, or product
___25. MAIMED   Y. Inattention

View From Saturday Vocabulary Matching 4 Answer Key

Y - 1. NEGLECT	A. Tiniest fraction of a second
D - 2. RENDERING	B. State of being semi-transparent
Q - 3. BRAWN	C. Decorate splendidly
B - 4. TRANSLUCENCE	D. Version or translation
H - 5. REVISED	E. Lingered without purpose
L - 6. INEVITABLE	F. Injured permanently
N - 7. TRAJECTORY	G. Small hill
K - 8. PERPETUAL	H. Reconsidered; altered; amended; improved
P - 9. PROTRUDING	I. List of the quantity of items contained in an area
W - 10. DISENTANGLED	J. Divided into smaller units
G - 11. KNOLL	K. Continuing without change or end
I - 12. INVENTORY	L. Certain; with an unavoidable outcome
S - 13. UNFURL	M. A point or limit
R - 14. COIFFED	N. Path a flying object takes
J - 15. PARCELED	O. Able to cut into fourths
U - 16. ADMONISH	P. Sticking out
V - 17. ANIMATED	Q. Physical strength
E - 18. HOVERED	R. Characterized by carefully styled, immaculate hairdo
M - 19. VERGE	S. Spread out from a folded position
C - 20. ADORN	T. Traveling
O - 21. QUARTERING	U. Warn
T - 22. ITINERANT	V. Lively
X - 23. CONVERSION	W. Untwisted
A - 24. NANOSECOND	X. Something that has changed into another form, substance, state, or product
F - 25. MAIMED	Y. Inattention

View From Saturday Vocabulary Magic Squares 1

Match the definition with the vocabulary word. Put your answers in the magic squares below. When your answers are correct, all columns and rows will add to the same number.

A. ADVISED
B. FAVORABLE
C. REINFORCE
D. NANOSECOND
E. VULGAR
F. AMBLED
G. QUARTERING
H. STRICT
I. PRECEDED
J. NONCHALANTLY
K. RUCKUS
L. INEVITABLE
M. UNFURL
N. CARAFE
O. BENEVOLENTLY
P. INCANDESCENTLY

1. Offered advice; recommended
2. Glass receptacle with an open top used for holding liquid
3. In a relaxed manner
4. Lacking charm, culture, or sophistication
5. Able to cut into fourths
6. Certain; with an unavoidable outcome
7. Glowingly
8. Strengthen
9. Kindly
10. Tiniest fraction of a second
11. Without relaxation or distraction
12. Commotion
13. To have gone before
14. Strolled or walked leisurely
15. Showing approval
16. Spread out from a folded position

A=	B=	C=	D=
E=	F=	G=	H=
I=	J=	K=	L=
M=	N=	O=	P=

View From Saturday Vocabulary Magic Squares 1 Answer Key

Match the definition with the vocabulary word. Put your answers in the magic squares below. When your answers are correct, all columns and rows will add to the same number.

A. ADVISED
B. FAVORABLE
C. REINFORCE
D. NANOSECOND
E. VULGAR
F. AMBLED
G. QUARTERING
H. STRICT
I. PRECEDED
J. NONCHALANTLY
K. RUCKUS
L. INEVITABLE
M. UNFURL
N. CARAFE
O. BENEVOLENTLY
P. INCANDESCENTLY

1. Offered advice; recommended
2. Glass receptacle with an open top used for holding liquid
3. In a relaxed manner
4. Lacking charm, culture, or sophistication
5. Able to cut into fourths
6. Certain; with an unavoidable outcome
7. Glowingly
8. Strengthen
9. Kindly
10. Tiniest fraction of a second
11. Without relaxation or distraction
12. Commotion
13. To have gone before
14. Strolled or walked leisurely
15. Showing approval
16. Spread out from a folded position

A=1	B=15	C=8	D=10
E=4	F=14	G=5	H=11
I=13	J=3	K=12	L=6
M=16	N=2	O=9	P=7

View From Saturday Vocabulary Magic Squares 2

Match the definition with the vocabulary word. Put your answers in the magic squares below. When your answers are correct, all columns and rows will add to the same number.

A. ACQUIRE
B. PARCELED
C. GENUS
D. ACCURATE
E. INVOLUNTARILY
F. CARAFE
G. FRIEZE
H. ADVISED
I. TRANQUILIZE
J. ITINERANT
K. INCUBATING
L. MALICE
M. PRECISION
N. BRAWN
O. SYLLABICATION
P. COMPLEMENTARY

1. Offered advice; recommended
2. To learn or possess
3. Divided into smaller units
4. Horizontal band of decoration in a building
5. Traveling
6. Having to do with the parts of words
7. Combining in such a way as to enhance each other
8. Administer a drug that will soothe or calm
9. Keeping eggs warm until hatchlings emerge
10. Physical strength
11. Exact in detail
12. Wanting to do harm
13. Doing something against one's will
14. Precisely correct
15. In biology, a category above species and below family
16. Glass receptacle with an open top used for holding liquid

A=	B=	C=	D=
E=	F=	G=	H=
I=	J=	K=	L=
M=	N=	O=	P=

View From Saturday Vocabulary Magic Squares 2 Answer Key

Match the definition with the vocabulary word. Put your answers in the magic squares below. When your answers are correct, all columns and rows will add to the same number.

A. ACQUIRE
B. PARCELED
C. GENUS
D. ACCURATE
E. INVOLUNTARILY
F. CARAFE
G. FRIEZE
H. ADVISED
I. TRANQUILIZE
J. ITINERANT
K. INCUBATING
L. MALICE
M. PRECISION
N. BRAWN
O. SYLLABICATION
P. COMPLEMENTARY

1. Offered advice; recommended
2. To learn or possess
3. Divided into smaller units
4. Horizontal band of decoration in a building
5. Traveling
6. Having to do with the parts of words
7. Combining in such a way as to enhance each other
8. Administer a drug that will soothe or calm
9. Keeping eggs warm until hatchlings emerge
10. Physical strength
11. Exact in detail
12. Wanting to do harm
13. Doing something against one's will
14. Precisely correct
15. In biology, a category above species and below family
16. Glass receptacle with an open top used for holding liquid

A=2	B=3	C=15	D=14
E=13	F=16	G=4	H=1
I=8	J=5	K=9	L=12
M=11	N=10	O=6	P=7

View From Saturday Vocabulary Magic Squares 3

Match the definition with the vocabulary word. Put your answers in the magic squares below. When your answers are correct, all columns and rows will add to the same number.

A. ECOLOGY
B. ACCURATE
C. INVOLUNTARILY
D. CAPSULE
E. MAMMOTH
F. PARCELED
G. GENUS
H. PRECEDED
I. CONCLUDED
J. STRICT
K. TRAJECTORY
L. EXCESSIVE
M. DECORUM
N. DEFINITELY
O. AMBLED
P. MEDIOCRE

1. Without doubt
2. In biology, a category above species and below family
3. More than is needed or wanted
4. Branch of biology examining the relationship of organisms to one another and their environment
5. Path a flying object takes
6. Precisely correct
7. Etiquette; proper social behavior
8. To have gone before
9. Huge
10. Average to below average in quality
11. Doing something against one's will
12. Without relaxation or distraction
13. Compact and succinct
14. Decided through reasoning and deliberation
15. Divided into smaller units
16. Strolled or walked leisurely

A=	B=	C=	D=
E=	F=	G=	H=
I=	J=	K=	L=
M=	N=	O=	P=

View From Saturday Vocabulary Magic Squares 3 Answer Key

Match the definition with the vocabulary word. Put your answers in the magic squares below. When your answers are correct, all columns and rows will add to the same number.

A. ECOLOGY
B. ACCURATE
C. INVOLUNTARILY
D. CAPSULE
E. MAMMOTH
F. PARCELED
G. GENUS
H. PRECEDED
I. CONCLUDED
J. STRICT
K. TRAJECTORY
L. EXCESSIVE
M. DECORUM
N. DEFINITELY
O. AMBLED
P. MEDIOCRE

1. Without doubt
2. In biology, a category above species and below family
3. More than is needed or wanted
4. Branch of biology examining the relationship of organisms to one another and their environment
5. Path a flying object takes
6. Precisely correct
7. Etiquette; proper social behavior
8. To have gone before
9. Huge
10. Average to below average in quality
11. Doing something against one's will
12. Without relaxation or distraction
13. Compact and succinct
14. Decided through reasoning and deliberation
15. Divided into smaller units
16. Strolled or walked leisurely

A=4	B=6	C=11	D=13
E=9	F=15	G=2	H=8
I=14	J=12	K=5	L=3
M=7	N=1	O=16	P=10

View From Saturday Vocabulary Magic Squares 4

Match the definition with the vocabulary word. Put your answers in the magic squares below. When your answers are correct, all columns and rows will add to the same number.

A. CONVERSION
B. CARAFE
C. EXCESSIVE
D. FEEBLE
E. ORIGINATE
F. PREOCCUPIED
G. DOMICILES
H. INEVITABLE
I. MAMMOTH
J. NEGLECT
K. TORMENT
L. TERMINALLY
M. MULTICULTURALISM
N. TRANSLUCENCE
O. MEDIOCRE
P. COMPLEMENTARY

1. Average to below average in quality
2. Weak
3. Inattention
4. Have a beginning
5. Huge
6. Consumed by the thought of something
7. Combining in such a way as to enhance each other
8. More than is needed or wanted
9. Certain; with an unavoidable outcome
10. Intense suffering
11. Something that has changed into another form, substance, state, or product
12. State of being semi-transparent
13. Glass receptacle with an open top used for holding liquid
14. Pertaining to a variety of cultural groups
15. Homes
16. Irreversibly

A=	B=	C=	D=
E=	F=	G=	H=
I=	J=	K=	L=
M=	N=	O=	P=

View From Saturday Vocabulary Magic Squares 4 Answer Key

Match the definition with the vocabulary word. Put your answers in the magic squares below. When your answers are correct, all columns and rows will add to the same number.

A. CONVERSION
B. CARAFE
C. EXCESSIVE
D. FEEBLE
E. ORIGINATE
F. PREOCCUPIED
G. DOMICILES
H. INEVITABLE
I. MAMMOTH
J. NEGLECT
K. TORMENT
L. TERMINALLY
M. MULTICULTURALISM
N. TRANSLUCENCE
O. MEDIOCRE
P. COMPLEMENTARY

1. Average to below average in quality
2. Weak
3. Inattention
4. Have a beginning
5. Huge
6. Consumed by the thought of something
7. Combining in such a way as to enhance each other
8. More than is needed or wanted
9. Certain; with an unavoidable outcome
10. Intense suffering
11. Something that has changed into another form, substance, state, or product
12. State of being semi-transparent
13. Glass receptacle with an open top used for holding liquid
14. Pertaining to a variety of cultural groups
15. Homes
16. Irreversibly

A=11	B=13	C=8	D=2
E=4	F=6	G=15	H=9
I=5	J=3	K=10	L=16
M=14	N=12	O=1	P=7

View From Saturday Vocabulary Word Search 1

```
C A P S U L E B E N E V O L E N T L Y J
Q V S E T N I O P P A B K V K T P A F T
P U P N E G L E C T H D Q N T N N B Y M
Y L O T C I R T S Z E A S V O I S L R S
X G N I P A R C E L E D L I M L L K U T
E A T N S H N Q G F B C S A B A L N C C
C R A E Y D G N H H J R T D N N K K F
O D N L V E A M Q R E E I I H X G L U F
L Q E S N T C X W V D M M R C R A S S M
O V O C N A O T N Y C R N Z O N T J A W
G Q U E L C N O D L E C W A I N N L D B
Y L S U O I C O R T A T A D F B I C O G
H I J N G T L M E N R N R V F C A C R K
D L D F E S U D I A A A B I E K U T N G
A V K U N I D E N L C L J S D F Q L E T
M R B R U H E F F A Q I C E L B E E F D
B A C L S P D A O H U B A D C L K T V N
L Y I H V O R C R C I U R W B T H P K L
E H Y M I S B T C N R J A G R G O F N G
D E G R E V G O E O E R F D E C O R U M
P R E C E D E D B N G I E R E V O S Y J
```

A point or limit (5)
Assign people to a certain task or job (7)
Branch of biology examining the relationship of organisms to one another and their environment (7)
Characterized by carefully styled, immaculate hairdo (7)
Charmingly old-fashioned (6)
Collection of historical documents or records (7)
Commotion (6)
Compact and succinct (7)
Decided through reasoning and deliberation (9)
Decorate splendidly (5)
Divided into smaller units (8)
Etiquette; proper social behavior (7)
Existing in fact (7)
Extremely badly (11)
Fundamental (8)
Glass receptacle with an open top used for holding liquid (6)
Guards (9)
Having worldly experience or culture (13)
In a relaxed manner (12)
In biology, a category above species and below family (5)
Inattention (7)
Injured permanently (6)
Irreversibly (10)
Kindly (12)
King who is supreme ruler (9)
Lacking charm, culture, or sophistication (6)
Lively (8)
Occurring in a manner opposite to what is expected (6)
Occurring without planning or warning (11)
Offered advice; recommended (7)
Path a flying object takes (10)
Physical strength (5)
Small hill (5)
Something that has changed into another form, substance, state, or product (10)
Spread out from a folded position (6)
Strengthen (9)
Strolled or walked leisurely (6)
Tapered off; became smaller or less (5)
To have gone before (8)
To learn or possess (7)
Triumphantly happy (8)
Unit of troops who stand closely together (7)
Untwisted (12)
Wanting to do harm (6)
Weak (6)
Without relaxation or distraction (6)

View From Saturday Vocabulary Word Search 1 Answer Key

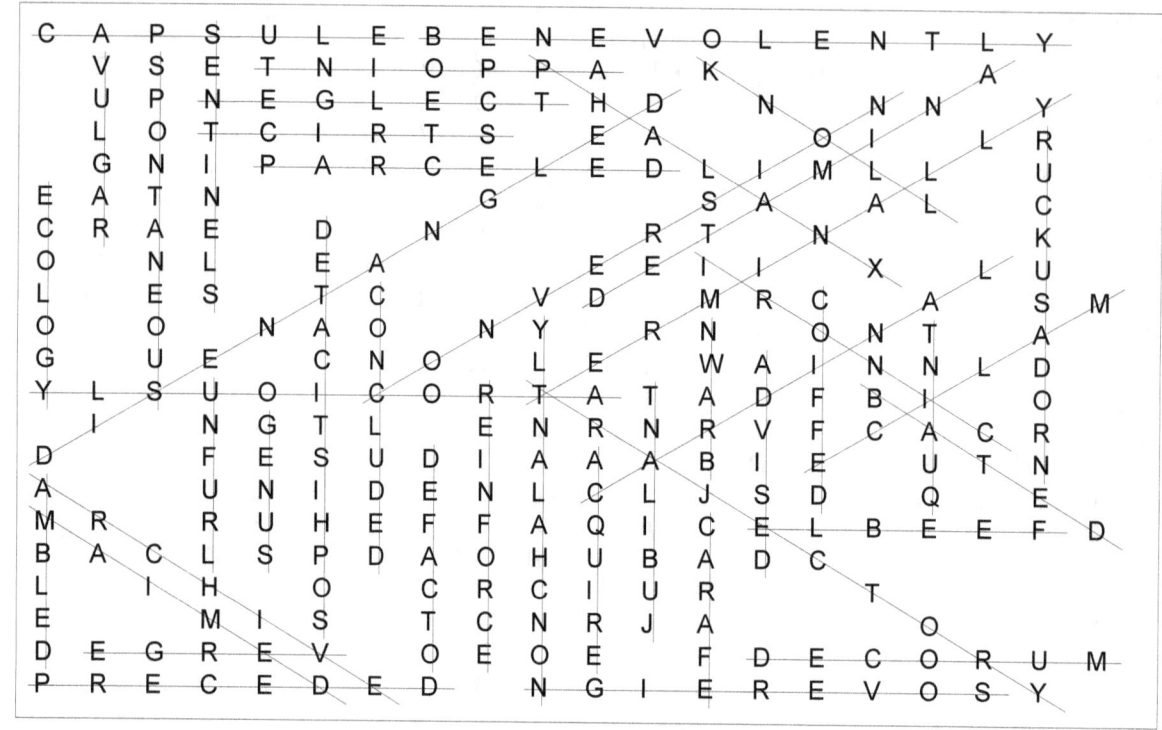

A point or limit (5)
Assign people to a certain task or job (7)
Branch of biology examining the relationship of organisms to one another and their environment (7)
Characterized by carefully styled, immaculate hairdo (7)
Charmingly old-fashioned (6)
Collection of historical documents or records (7)
Commotion (6)
Compact and succinct (7)
Decided through reasoning and deliberation (9)
Decorate splendidly (5)
Divided into smaller units (8)
Etiquette; proper social behavior (7)
Existing in fact (7)
Extremely badly (11)
Fundamental (8)
Glass receptacle with an open top used for holding liquid (6)
Guards (9)
Having worldly experience or culture (13)
In a relaxed manner (12)
In biology, a category above species and below family (5)
Inattention (7)
Injured permanently (6)

Irreversibly (10)
Kindly (12)
King who is supreme ruler (9)
Lacking charm, culture, or sophistication (6)
Lively (8)
Occurring in a manner opposite to what is expected (6)
Occurring without planning or warning (11)
Offered advice; recommended (7)
Path a flying object takes (10)
Physical strength (5)
Small hill (5)
Something that has changed into another form, substance, state, or product (10)
Spread out from a folded position (6)
Strengthen (9)
Strolled or walked leisurely (6)
Tapered off; became smaller or less (5)
To have gone before (8)
To learn or possess (7)
Triumphantly happy (8)
Unit of troops who stand closely together (7)
Untwisted (12)
Wanting to do harm (6)
Weak (6)
Without relaxation or distraction (6)

View From Saturday Vocabulary Word Search 2

```
I K Z C A A S G N I R E D N E R K M N P
N X B T H D N O S M Y N O R C A W U E J
V G E N U S M I V H R I K H L J M L G Y
E V S I Y Y M O M E T X E T E R P T L C
N U C O K P O D N A R S U K C U R I E Y
T L O P J T S X Z I T E K N T R Y C C D
O G I P C N X I F A S E I H E R C U T Z
R A F A M I L L B R S H D G R O B L Y V
Y R F L Q A P R E C I S I O N Q D T S L
G E E R R U L R B H O K Q C L E I U C P
D Z D U I Q C I H I J N L V I S O R A C
X F T F R E M Y C V D U V P R E V A R R
V A L N O R Z Z F E D E U E N D E L D M
N E S U N T W E L E F C V A R T J I I K
A Y R D I C G E D A C I T V A S D S N V
C M R G C I C B R O D N E N K E I M A Y
Q A B P E R B A E F O L I Q R N N O L L
U I A L A T C R J P B G V E W R O U N G
I M T P E S P Z S E I V V A O F R L Y S
R E E D E D E C E R P O R D Y N C G L K
E D D M L T H F O S H B A M U R O C E D
```

A point or limit (5)
Assign people to a certain task or job (7)
Characterized by carefully styled, immaculate hairdo (7)
Charmingly old-fashioned (6)
Collection of historical documents or records (7)
Commotion (6)
Consumed by the thought of something (11)
Decided through reasoning and deliberation (9)
Decorate splendidly (5)
Divided into smaller units (8)
Etiquette; proper social behavior (7)
Exact in detail (9)
Existing in fact (7)
False excuse (7)
Fundamental (8)
Glass receptacle with an open top used for holding liquid (6)
Hard to control (6)
Have a beginning (9)
Horizontal band of decoration in a building (6)
In biology, a category above species and below family (5)
Inattention (7)
Injured permanently (6)
King who is supreme ruler (9)
Lacking charm, culture, or sophistication (6)
Lingered without purpose (7)
List of the quantity of items contained in an area (9)
Lively (8)
Occurring in a manner opposite to what is expected (6)
Occurring without planning or warning (11)
Pertaining to a variety of cultural groups (16)
Physical strength (5)
Podium (7)
Process of granting citizenship to a foreigner (14)
Small hill (5)
Something that has changed into another form, substance, state, or product (10)
Spread out from a folded position (6)
Strolled or walked leisurely (6)
Tapered off; became smaller or less (5)
To have gone before (8)
To learn or possess (7)
Variety (9)
Version or translation (9)
Wanting to do harm (6)
Warn (8)
Weak (6)
Without relaxation or distraction (6)
Word created from the initial letters of words in a longer phrase (8)

View From Saturday Vocabulary Word Search 2 Answer Key

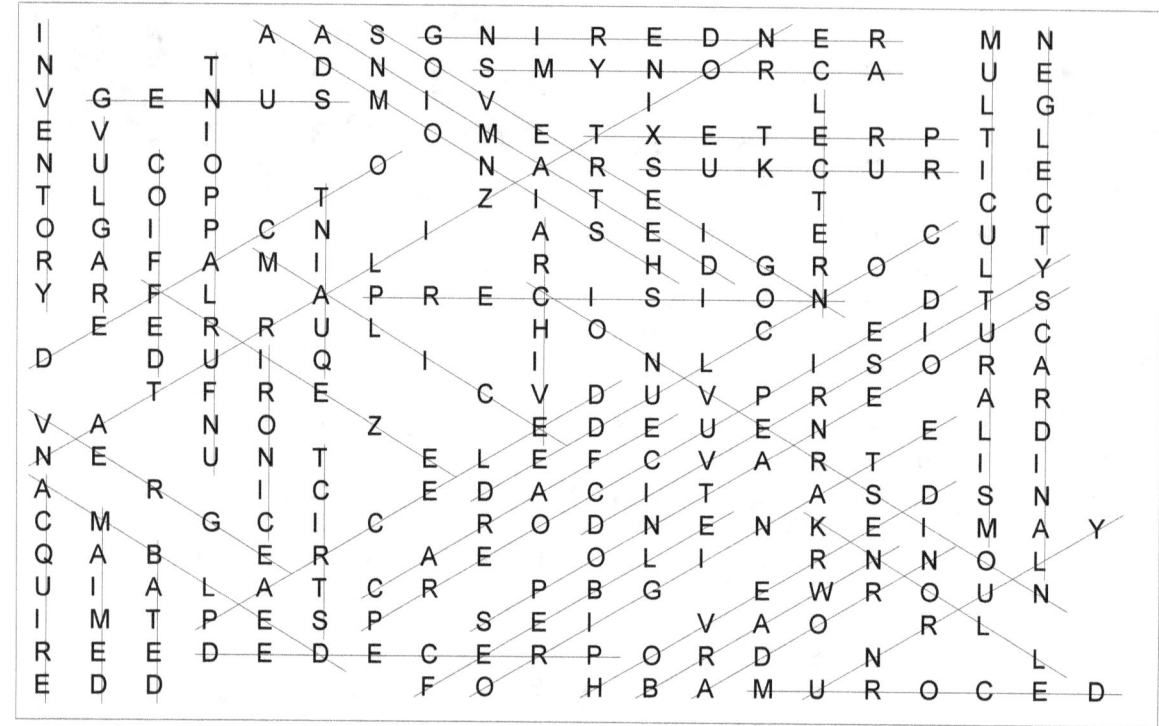

A point or limit (5)
Assign people to a certain task or job (7)
Characterized by carefully styled, immaculate hairdo (7)
Charmingly old-fashioned (6)
Collection of historical documents or records (7)
Commotion (6)
Consumed by the thought of something (11)
Decided through reasoning and deliberation (9)
Decorate splendidly (5)
Divided into smaller units (8)
Etiquette; proper social behavior (7)
Exact in detail (9)
Existing in fact (7)
False excuse (7)
Fundamental (8)
Glass receptacle with an open top used for holding liquid (6)
Hard to control (6)
Have a beginning (9)
Horizontal band of decoration in a building (6)
In biology, a category above species and below family (5)
Inattention (7)
Injured permanently (6)
King who is supreme ruler (9)
Lacking charm, culture, or sophistication (6)

Lingered without purpose (7)
List of the quantity of items contained in an area (9)
Lively (8)
Occurring in a manner opposite to what is expected (6)
Occurring without planning or warning (11)
Pertaining to a variety of cultural groups (16)
Physical strength (5)
Podium (7)
Process of granting citizenship to a foreigner (14)
Small hill (5)
Something that has changed into another form, substance, state, or product (10)
Spread out from a folded position (6)
Strolled or walked leisurely (6)
Tapered off; became smaller or less (5)
To have gone before (8)
To learn or possess (7)
Variety (9)
Version or translation (9)
Wanting to do harm (6)
Warn (8)
Weak (6)
Without relaxation or distraction (6)
Word created from the initial letters of words in a longer phrase (8)

View From Saturday Vocabulary Word Search 3

```
R U C K U S I N C U B A T I N G D C Y Y
R T N E D E C E R P S D R P D E M A R D
P C S S E D A Y G O L O C E F D A R S Z
A R M Z T I M T N G N H F F Z E L A O Q
N C E A A V R C R I H I I Z F F I F V Y
I A C C C E C Z C O N O M F D A C E E F
M P H Q I R K R V I C L U R N C E Z R D
A S A U T S T S T E E I R D O T P E E Q
T U N I S I I E D C R L O D C O V T I F
E L I R I T L O T U E G C U E I A V G W
D E S E H Y S E N T I N E L S B Y U N W
R L M M P T R R A O E R D S O L B L R P
P M T Q O N U N L N N R E P N W Y G O Y
C H E D S L I C I T T C M I A K C A D S
M T A D Y G C O B C X D H I N O N R A V
U O Y L I V G N U E N B P A N F L O P D
N M R R A O T V J L B Q R V L A O N L Z
F M O B C N C E V G B D E A U A L R P L
U A T A R B X R V E B R C T W V N L C V
R M C D O T M G E N S M E A M N E T Y E
L D E V N P A E G I T P D J M Z G S L H
L M J I Y K I D O W R J E T E B U P Y Y
D F A S M Y M N D E I X D I K N L Y J X
Z U R E S B E Y P V C D R R E L B E E F
Q Q T D X R D M P S T F Z G G H X D D D
```

ACQUIRE	COIFFED	GENUS	NANOSECOND	RUCKUS
ACRONYMS	CONVERGED	INCUBATING	NEGLECT	SENTINELS
ADORN	CONVERSION	IRONIC	NONCHALANTLY	SOPHISTICATED
ADVISED	DECORUM	JUBILANT	ORIGINATE	SOVEREIGN
AMBLED	DEFACTO	KNOLL	PERPETUAL	STRICT
ANIMATED	DEFINITELY	LECTERN	PHALANX	TERMINALLY
ATROCIOUSLY	DIVERSITY	MAIMED	PRECEDED	TRAJECTORY
BATED	ECOLOGY	MALICE	PRECEDENT	UNFURL
BRAWN	EXCESSIVE	MAMMOTH	PRECISION	UNRULY
CAPSULE	FEEBLE	MECHANISM	QUAINT	VERGE
CARAFE	FRIEZE	MEDIOCRE	REINFORCE	VULGAR

View From Saturday Vocabulary Word Search 3 Answer Key

ACQUIRE	COIFFED	GENUS	NANOSECOND	RUCKUS
ACRONYMS	CONVERGED	INCUBATING	NEGLECT	SENTINELS
ADORN	CONVERSION	IRONIC	NONCHALANTLY	SOPHISTICATED
ADVISED	DECORUM	JUBILANT	ORIGINATE	SOVEREIGN
AMBLED	DEFACTO	KNOLL	PERPETUAL	STRICT
ANIMATED	DEFINITELY	LECTERN	PHALANX	TERMINALLY
ATROCIOUSLY	DIVERSITY	MAIMED	PRECEDED	TRAJECTORY
BATED	ECOLOGY	MALICE	PRECEDENT	UNFURL
BRAWN	EXCESSIVE	MAMMOTH	PRECISION	UNRULY
CAPSULE	FEEBLE	MECHANISM	QUAINT	VERGE
CARAFE	FRIEZE	MEDIOCRE	REINFORCE	VULGAR

View From Saturday Vocabulary Word Search 4

```
T L A C Q U I R E C O L O G Y T F C W T
O E K F U U I N V E N T O R Y S E O T L
R C N X A M A M M O T H E D E Y E N J C
M T O O R I G I N A T E V L H N B V I D
E E L T T I R O N N I C D I G O O L E N W
N R L H E C M L X T E C H N V I E R C X
T N X J R A N P X T I K C R E S Z G U L
T P J T I P E R A M Y H R G R R C E B X
E G E M N S G B O K A Q A A E E L D A V
R P E R G U L D C L V M M P D V A U T B
M D V C P L E T A R L D S P J N N N I D
I H M O M E C N R H E G G O O O I F N L
N Y L I R A T N U L O V N I D C D U G Z
A D D F N L N U G M S V T N X E R R Z Z
L E Q F Y Z S N A A V A B T D Q A L H F
L C R E F R A D D L Z U G U C J C E K M
Y O I D A T E Z E I R F L P H A L A N X
J R V T N S L M L C V C R G D B R W M V
W U Q E I C C A N E N E V O A V A A O F
N M S V M N R K L O C Q R T D R B T F D
N I D D A U E G C E T N I S B W C V E E
D A Z B T Z Q R D L V V U H I A P L G N
P Q F A E L M E A D E N Z Z F T B Y R N
B G N L D N N T W N E S Y E Z M Y P E B
S T R I C T C Z I G T N D K A V R F V J
```

ACQUIRE	CONCLUDED	INCUBATING	NONCHALANTLY
ADORN	CONVERGED	INEVITABLE	ORIGINATE
ADVISED	CONVERSION	INVENTORY	PERPETUAL
AMBLED	DECORUM	INVOLUNTARILY	PHALANX
ANIMATED	DEFACTO	IRONIC	PRECEDENT
APPOINT	DISENTANGLED	ITINERANT	QUAINT
ARCHIVE	DIVERSITY	KNOLL	QUARTERING
BATED	DOMICILES	LECTERN	STRICT
BRAWN	ECOLOGY	MAIMED	TERMINALLY
CAPSULE	FEEBLE	MALICE	TORMENT
CARAFE	FRIEZE	MAMMOTH	UNFURL
CARDINAL	GENUS	NATURALIZATION	VERGE
COIFFED	HOVERED	NEGLECT	VULGAR

View From Saturday Vocabulary Word Search 4 Answer Key

ACQUIRE	CONCLUDED	INCUBATING	NONCHALANTLY
ADORN	CONVERGED	INEVITABLE	ORIGINATE
ADVISED	CONVERSION	INVENTORY	PERPETUAL
AMBLED	DECORUM	INVOLUNTARILY	PHALANX
ANIMATED	DEFACTO	IRONIC	PRECEDENT
APPOINT	DISENTANGLED	ITINERANT	QUAINT
ARCHIVE	DIVERSITY	KNOLL	QUARTERING
BATED	DOMICILES	LECTERN	STRICT
BRAWN	ECOLOGY	MAIMED	TERMINALLY
CAPSULE	FEEBLE	MALICE	TORMENT
CARAFE	FRIEZE	MAMMOTH	UNFURL
CARDINAL	GENUS	NATURALIZATION	VERGE
COIFFED	HOVERED	NEGLECT	VULGAR

View From Saturday Vocabulary Crossword 1

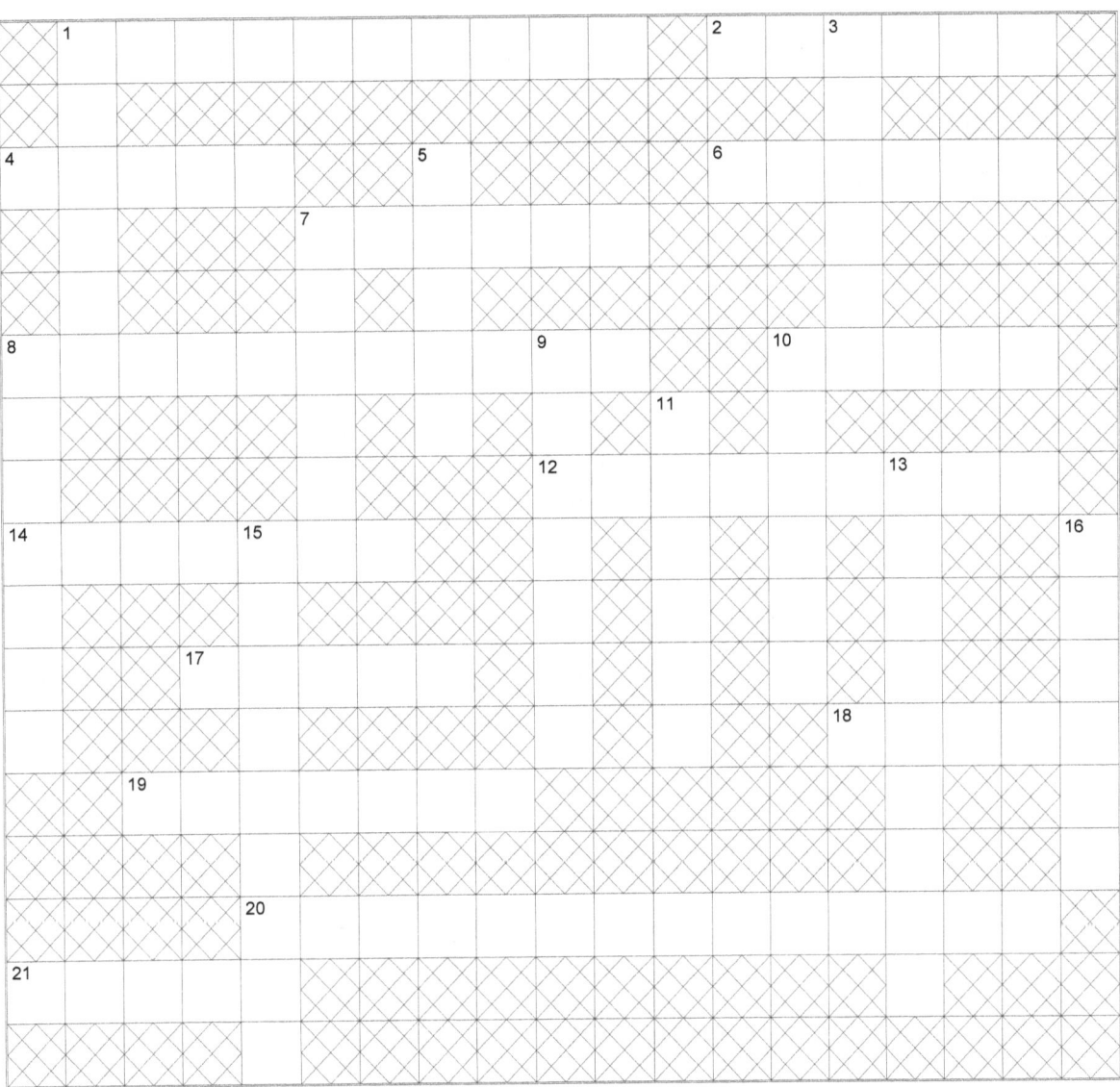

Across
1. Able to cut into fourths
2. Commotion
4. Tapered off; became smaller or less
6. Hard to control
7. Weak
8. Extremely badly
10. A point or limit
12. Decided through reasoning and deliberation
14. Lingered without purpose
17. Small hill
18. Physical strength
19. False excuse
20. Glowingly
21. Decorate splendidly

Down
1. Charmingly old-fashioned
3. Glass receptacle with an open top used for holding liquid
5. In biology, a category above species and below family
7. Horizontal band of decoration in a building
8. Collection of historical documents or records
9. Podium
10. Lacking charm, culture, or sophistication
11. Spread out from a folded position
13. Variety
15. Version or translation
16. Occurring in a manner opposite to what is expected

View From Saturday Vocabulary Crossword 1 Answer Key

Across
1. Able to cut into fourths
2. Commotion
4. Tapered off; became smaller or less
6. Hard to control
7. Weak
8. Extremely badly
10. A point or limit
12. Decided through reasoning and deliberation
14. Lingered without purpose
17. Small hill
18. Physical strength
19. False excuse
20. Glowingly
21. Decorate splendidly

Down
1. Charmingly old-fashioned
3. Glass receptacle with an open top used for holding liquid
5. In biology, a category above species and below family
7. Horizontal band of decoration in a building
8. Collection of historical documents or records
9. Podium
10. Lacking charm, culture, or sophistication
11. Spread out from a folded position
13. Variety
15. Version or translation
16. Occurring in a manner opposite to what is expected

View From Saturday Vocabulary Crossword 2

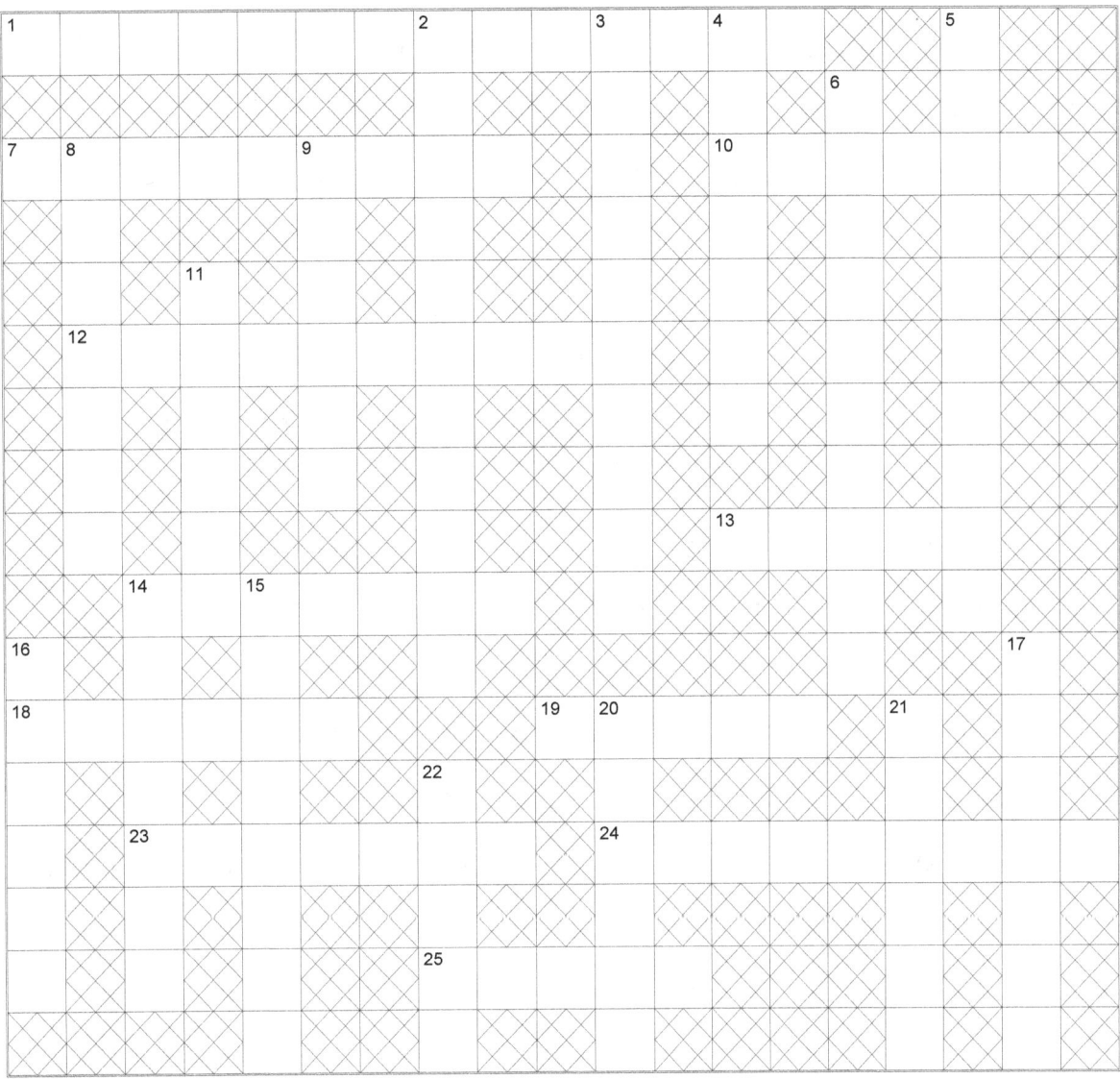

Across
1. Glowingly
7. Exact in detail
10. Glass receptacle with an open top used for holding liquid
12. Certain; with an unavoidable outcome
13. Small hill
14. Etiquette; proper social behavior
18. Spread out from a folded position
19. Physical strength
23. Characterized by carefully styled, immaculate hairdo
24. Came from different directions toward a central point
25. In biology, a category above species and below family

Down
2. Occurring without planning or warning
3. Tiniest fraction of a second
4. Podium
5. Without doubt
6. Path a flying object takes
8. Reconsidered; altered; amended; improved
9. Without relaxation or distraction
11. Weak
14. Existing in fact
15. Fundamental
16. Charmingly old-fashioned
17. Lingered without purpose
20. Commotion
21. Hard to control
22. A point or limit

View From Saturday Vocabulary Crossword 2 Answer Key

Across
1. Glowingly
7. Exact in detail
10. Glass receptacle with an open top used for holding liquid
12. Certain; with an unavoidable outcome
13. Small hill
14. Etiquette; proper social behavior
18. Spread out from a folded position
19. Physical strength
23. Characterized by carefully styled, immaculate hairdo
24. Came from different directions toward a central point
25. In biology, a category above species and below family

Down
2. Occurring without planning or warning
3. Tiniest fraction of a second
4. Podium
5. Without doubt
6. Path a flying object takes
8. Reconsidered; altered; amended; improved
9. Without relaxation or distraction
11. Weak
14. Existing in fact
15. Fundamental
16. Charmingly old-fashioned
17. Lingered without purpose
20. Commotion
21. Hard to control
22. A point or limit

View From Saturday Vocabulary Crossword 3

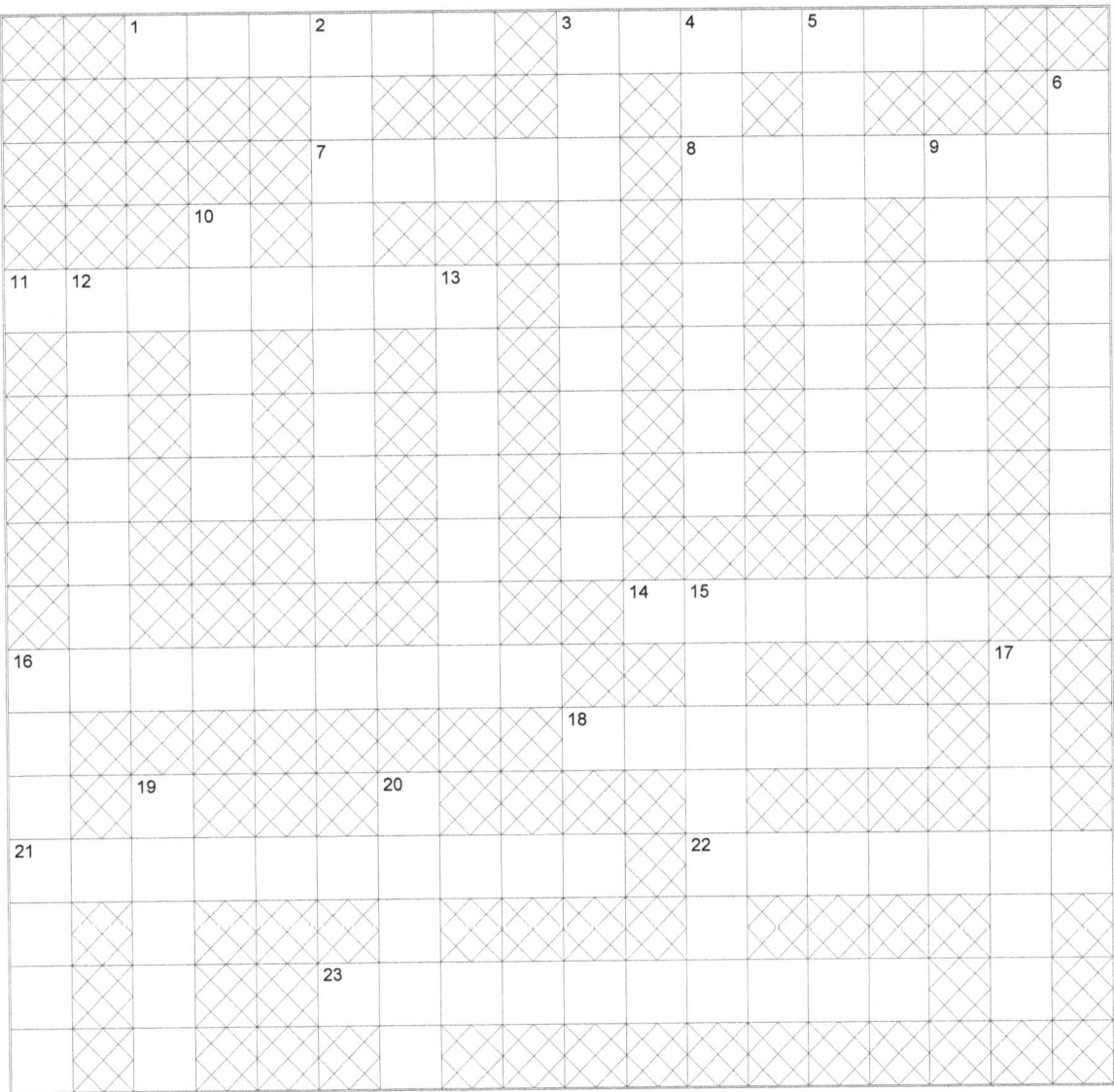

Across
1. Wanting to do harm
3. Unit of troops who stand closely together
7. A point or limit
8. Characterized by carefully styled, immaculate hairdo
11. Fundamental
14. Without relaxation or distraction
16. Version or translation
18. Glass receptacle with an open top used for holding liquid
21. Certain; with an unavoidable outcome
22. Branch of biology examining the relationship of organisms to one another and their environment
23. Without doubt

Down
2. List of the quantity of items contained in an area
3. Exact in detail
4. Precisely correct
5. Lively
6. Warn
9. Weak
10. Decorate splendidly
12. To learn or possess
13. Podium
15. Intense suffering
16. Reconsidered; altered; amended; improved
17. Lacking charm, culture, or sophistication
19. In biology, a category above species and below family
20. Tapered off; became smaller or less

View From Saturday Vocabulary Crossword 3 Answer Key

Across
1. Wanting to do harm
3. Unit of troops who stand closely together
7. A point or limit
8. Characterized by carefully styled, immaculate hairdo
11. Fundamental
14. Without relaxation or distraction
16. Version or translation
18. Glass receptacle with an open top used for holding liquid
21. Certain; with an unavoidable outcome
22. Branch of biology examining the relationship of organisms to one another and their environment
23. Without doubt

Down
2. List of the quantity of items contained in an area
3. Exact in detail
4. Precisely correct
5. Lively
6. Warn
9. Weak
10. Decorate splendidly
12. To learn or possess
13. Podium
15. Intense suffering
16. Reconsidered; altered; amended; improved
17. Lacking charm, culture, or sophistication
19. In biology, a category above species and below family
20. Tapered off; became smaller or less

View From Saturday Vocabulary Crossword 4

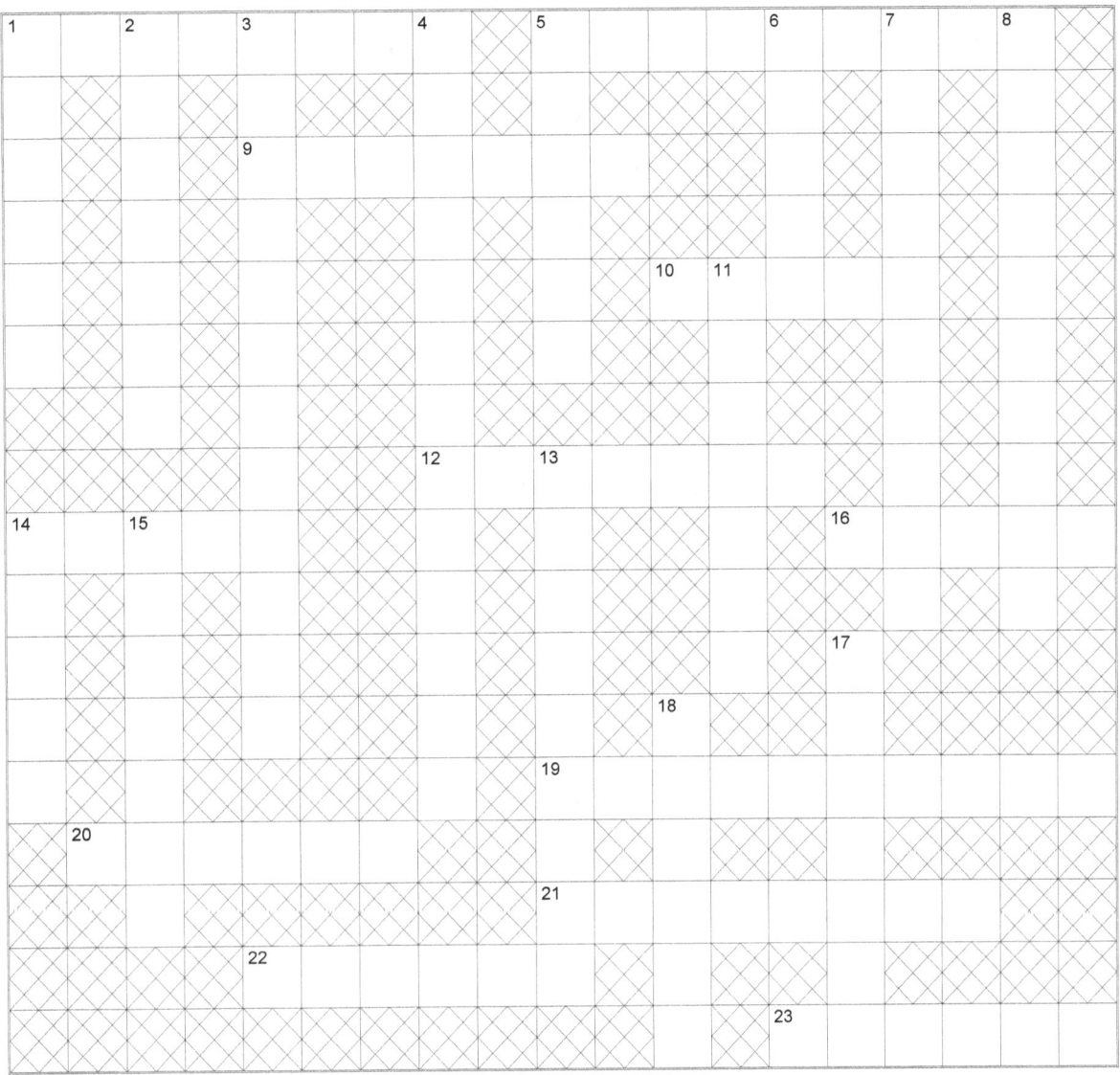

Across
1. Word created from the initial letters of words in a longer phrase
5. Kept oneself from doing something
9. Inattention
10. In biology, a category above species and below family
12. Compact and succinct
14. Physical strength
16. Small hill
19. Path a flying object takes
20. Occurring in a manner opposite to what is expected
21. Warn
22. Spread out from a folded position
23. Weak

Down
1. Strolled or walked leisurely
2. Reconsidered; altered; amended; improved
3. In a relaxed manner
4. Having to do with the parts of words
5. Commotion
6. Decorate splendidly
7. Tiniest fraction of a second
8. Without doubt
11. Branch of biology examining the relationship of organisms to one another and their environment
13. Continuing without change or end
14. Tapered off; became smaller or less
15. To learn or possess
17. Collection of historical documents or records
18. Injured permanently

View From Saturday Vocabulary Crossword 4 Answer Key

Across
1. Word created from the initial letters of words in a longer phrase
5. Kept oneself from doing something
9. Inattention
10. In biology, a category above species and below family
12. Compact and succinct
14. Physical strength
16. Small hill
19. Path a flying object takes
20. Occurring in a manner opposite to what is expected
21. Warn
22. Spread out from a folded position
23. Weak

Down
1. Strolled or walked leisurely
2. Reconsidered; altered; amended; improved
3. In a relaxed manner
4. Having to do with the parts of words
5. Commotion
6. Decorate splendidly
7. Tiniest fraction of a second
8. Without doubt
11. Branch of biology examining the relationship of organisms to one another and their environment
13. Continuing without change or end
14. Tapered off; became smaller or less
15. To learn or possess
17. Collection of historical documents or records
18. Injured permanently

View From Saturday Vocabulary Juggle Letters 1

1. URMEDOC = 1. _____
Etiquette; proper social behavior

2. EGIITONAR = 2. _____
Have a beginning

3. IERACVH = 3. _____
Collection of historical documents or records

4. LPAXHNA = 4. _____
Unit of troops who stand closely together

5. LMETYNARIL = 5. _____
Irreversibly

6. LKONL = 6. _____
Small hill

7. NEAITRGURQ = 7. _____
Able to cut into fourths

8. IXVEEESSC = 8. _____
More than is needed or wanted

9. LVARGU = 9. _____
Lacking charm, culture, or sophistication

10. ENTIADAM =10. _____
Lively

11. IOFCDFE =11. _____
Characterized by carefully styled, immaculate hairdo

12. PREMTOANEMYCL =12. _____
Combining in such a way as to enhance each other

13. UURCKS =13. _____
Commotion

14. GENTELC =14. _____
Inattention

15. TITNINARE =15. _____
Traveling

View From Saturday Vocabulary Juggle Letters 1 Answer Key

1. URMEDOC = 1. DECORUM
Etiquette; proper social behavior

2. EGIITONAR = 2. ORIGINATE
Have a beginning

3. IERACVH = 3. ARCHIVE
Collection of historical documents or records

4. LPAXHNA = 4. PHALANX
Unit of troops who stand closely together

5. LMETYNARIL = 5. TERMINALLY
Irreversibly

6. LKONL = 6. KNOLL
Small hill

7. NEAITRGURQ = 7. QUARTERING
Able to cut into fourths

8. IXVEEESSC = 8. EXCESSIVE
More than is needed or wanted

9. LVARGU = 9. VULGAR
Lacking charm, culture, or sophistication

10. ENTIADAM =10. ANIMATED
Lively

11. IOFCDFE =11. COIFFED
Characterized by carefully styled, immaculate hairdo

12. PREMTOANEMYCL =12. COMPLEMENTARY
Combining in such a way as to enhance each other

13. UURCKS =13. RUCKUS
Commotion

14. GENTELC =14. NEGLECT
Inattention

15. TITNINARE =15. ITINERANT
Traveling

View From Saturday Vocabulary Juggle Letters 2

1. ALOINALYBSTIC = 1. _____
   Having to do with the parts of words

2. OSANSNPTUOE = 2. _____
   Occurring without planning or warning

3. IANMEATD = 3. _____
   Lively

4. CSPOIIENR = 4. _____
   Exact in detail

5. HANSIDOM = 5. _____
   Warn

6. SIMOLCIED = 6. _____
   Homes

7. YNULRU = 7. _____
   Hard to control

8. HINSEACMM = 8. _____
   Method or instinct an animal has for finding its way

9. ITRLDAITACO = 9. _____
   Behaving as if one has complete rule over others

10. CQIURAE = 10. _____
    To learn or possess

11. ENTIATNRI = 11. _____
    Traveling

12. IARRGQNETU = 12. _____
    Able to cut into fourths

13. NGUSE = 13. _____
    In biology, a category above species and below family

14. EUATELPRP = 14. _____
    Continuing without change or end

15. ETEANLSDDING = 15. _____
    Untwisted

View From Saturday Vocabulary Juggle Letters 2 Answer Key

1. ALOINALYBSTIC = 1. SYLLABICATION
Having to do with the parts of words

2. OSANSNPTUOE = 2. SPONTANEOUS
Occurring without planning or warning

3. IANMEATD = 3. ANIMATED
Lively

4. CSPOIIENR = 4. PRECISION
Exact in detail

5. HANSIDOM = 5. ADMONISH
Warn

6. SIMOLCIED = 6. DOMICILES
Homes

7. YNULRU = 7. UNRULY
Hard to control

8. HINSEACMM = 8. MECHANISM
Method or instinct an animal has for finding its way

9. ITRLDAITACO = 9. DICTATORIAL
Behaving as if one has complete rule over others

10. CQIURAE =10. ACQUIRE
To learn or possess

11. ENTIATNRI =11. ITINERANT
Traveling

12. IARRGQNETU =12. QUARTERING
Able to cut into fourths

13. NGUSE =13. GENUS
In biology, a category above species and below family

14. EUATELPRP =14. PERPETUAL
Continuing without change or end

15. ETEANLSDDING =15. DISENTANGLED
Untwisted

View From Saturday Vocabulary Juggle Letters 3

1. HSIAMNOD = 1. _____
   Warn

2. VINCERNSOO = 2. _____
   Something that has changed into another form, substance, state, or product

3. ECLMIA = 3. _____
   Wanting to do harm

4. GNEURTAIRQ = 4. _____
   Able to cut into fourths

5. EENRINDRG = 5. _____
   Version or translation

6. REOTNGIAI = 6. _____
   Have a beginning

7. AIMMDE = 7. _____
   Injured permanently

8. TYSIVEIDR = 8. _____
   Variety

9. UOEEPCCPIRD = 9. _____
   Consumed by the thought of something

10. YAEROTTJRC = 10. _____
    Path a flying object takes

11. TREPEULAP = 11. _____
    Continuing without change or end

12. CEDFATO = 12. _____
    Existing in fact

13. RTOVIEYNN = 13. _____
    List of the quantity of items contained in an area

14. EGEVR = 14. _____
    A point or limit

15. ARLNIUTLIVNOY = 15. _____
    Doing something against one's will

View From Saturday Vocabulary Juggle Letters 3 Answer Key

1. HSIAMNOD = 1. ADMONISH
Warn

2. VINCERNSOO = 2. CONVERSION
Something that has changed into another form, substance, state, or product

3. ECLMIA = 3. MALICE
Wanting to do harm

4. GNEURTAIRQ = 4. QUARTERING
Able to cut into fourths

5. EENRINDRG = 5. RENDERING
Version or translation

6. REOTNGIAI = 6. ORIGINATE
Have a beginning

7. AIMMDE = 7. MAIMED
Injured permanently

8. TYSIVEIDR = 8. DIVERSITY
Variety

9. UOEEPCCPIRD = 9. PREOCCUPIED
Consumed by the thought of something

10. YAEROTTJRC = 10. TRAJECTORY
Path a flying object takes

11. TREPEULAP = 11. PERPETUAL
Continuing without change or end

12. CEDFATO = 12. DEFACTO
Existing in fact

13. RTOVIEYNN = 13. INVENTORY
List of the quantity of items contained in an area

14. EGEVR = 14. VERGE
A point or limit

15. ARLNIUTLIVNOY = 15. INVOLUNTARILY
Doing something against one's will

View From Saturday Vocabulary Juggle Letters 4

1. MERUODC = 1. _____
   Etiquette; proper social behavior

2. NIIREAGOT = 2. _____
   Have a beginning

3. TCRELNE = 3. _____
   Podium

4. EEELBF = 4. _____
   Weak

5. VYOTEINNR = 5. _____
   List of the quantity of items contained in an area

6. SOLAIYCLATINB = 6. _____
   Having to do with the parts of words

7. CHTETDPSOISAI = 7. _____
   Having worldly experience or culture

8. PSAONEUOSNT = 8. _____
   Occurring without planning or warning

9. GNUSE = 9. _____
   In biology, a category above species and below family

10. RVIETDYSI =10. _____
    Variety

11. EIEXESVCS =11. _____
    More than is needed or wanted

12. UPLRPATEE =12. _____
    Continuing without change or end

13. ESANINTGEDDL =13. _____
    Untwisted

14. ENETLONBLVEY =14. _____
    Kindly

15. ZEFIER =15. _____
    Horizontal band of decoration in a building

View From Saturday Vocabulary Juggle Letters 4 Answer Key

1. MERUODC = 1. DECORUM
Etiquette; proper social behavior

2. NIIREAGOT = 2. ORIGINATE
Have a beginning

3. TCRELNE = 3. LECTERN
Podium

4. EEELBF = 4. FEEBLE
Weak

5. VYOTEINNR = 5. INVENTORY
List of the quantity of items contained in an area

6. SOLAIYCLATINB = 6. SYLLABICATION
Having to do with the parts of words

7. CHTETDPSOISAI = 7. SOPHISTICATED
Having worldly experience or culture

8. PSAONEUOSNT = 8. SPONTANEOUS
Occurring without planning or warning

9. GNUSE = 9. GENUS
In biology, a category above species and below family

10. RVIETDYSI =10. DIVERSITY
Variety

11. EIEXESVCS =11. EXCESSIVE
More than is needed or wanted

12. UPLRPATEE =12. PERPETUAL
Continuing without change or end

13. ESANINTGEDDL =13. DISENTANGLED
Untwisted

14. ENETLONBLVEY =14. BENEVOLENTLY
Kindly

15. ZEFIER =15. FRIEZE
Horizontal band of decoration in a building

Copyrighted

ACCURATE	Precisely correct
ACQUIRE	To learn or possess
ACRONYMS	Word created from the initial letters of words in a longer phrase
ADMONISH	Warn
ADORN	Decorate splendidly

ADVISED	Offered advice; recommended
AMBLED	Strolled or walked leisurely
ANIMATED	Lively
APPOINT	Assign people to a certain task or job
ARCHIVE	Collection of historical documents or records

ATROCIOUSLY	Extremely badly
BATED	Tapered off; became smaller or less
BENEVOLENTLY	Kindly
BRAWN	Physical strength
CAPSULE	Compact and succinct

CARAFE	Glass receptacle with an open top used for holding liquid
CARDINAL	Fundamental
COIFFED	Characterized by carefully styled, immaculate hairdo
COMPLEMENTARY	Combining in such a way as to enhance each other
CONCLUDED	Decided through reasoning and deliberation

CONVERGED	Came from different directions toward a central point
CONVERSION	Something that has changed into another form, substance, state, or product
DECORUM	Etiquette; proper social behavior
DEFACTO	Existing in fact
DEFINITELY	Without doubt

DICTATORIAL	Behaving as if one has complete rule over others
DISENTANGLED	Untwisted
DIVERSITY	Variety
DOMICILES	Homes
ECOLOGY	Branch of biology examining the relationship of organisms to one another and their environment

EXCESSIVE	More than is needed or wanted
FAVORABLE	Showing approval
FEEBLE	Weak
FRIEZE	Horizontal band of decoration in a building
GENUS	In biology, a category above species and below family

HOVERED	Lingered without purpose
INCANDESCENTLY	Glowingly
INCUBATING	Keeping eggs warm until hatchlings emerge
INEVITABLE	Certain; with an unavoidable outcome
INVENTORY	List of the quantity of items contained in an area

INVOLUNTARILY	Doing something against one's will
IRONIC	Occurring in a manner opposite to what is expected
ITINERANT	Traveling
JUBILANT	Triumphantly happy
KNOLL	Small hill

LECTERN	Podium
MAIMED	Injured permanently
MALICE	Wanting to do harm
MAMMOTH	Huge
MECHANISM	Method or instinct an animal has for finding its way

MEDIOCRE	Average to below average in quality
MULTICULTURALISM	Pertaining to a variety of cultural groups
NANOSECOND	Tiniest fraction of a second
NATURALIZATION	Process of granting citizenship to a foreigner
NEGLECT	Inattention

NONCHALANTLY	In a relaxed manner
ORIGINATE	Have a beginning
PARCELED	Divided into smaller units
PERPETUAL	Continuing without change or end
PHALANX	Unit of troops who stand closely together

PRECEDED	To have gone before
PRECEDENT	Previous event that serves as an example in the future
PRECISION	Exact in detail
PREOCCUPIED	Consumed by the thought of something
PRETEXT	False excuse

PROTRUDING	Sticking out
QUAINT	Charmingly old-fashioned
QUARTERING	Able to cut into fourths
REFRAINED	Kept oneself from doing something
REINFORCE	Strengthen

RENDERING	Version or translation
REVISED	Reconsidered; altered; amended; improved
RUCKUS	Commotion
SENTINELS	Guards
SOPHISTICATED	Having worldly experience or culture

SOVEREIGN	King who is supreme ruler
SPONTANEOUS	Occurring without planning or warning
STRICT	Without relaxation or distraction
SUPPRESSED	Prevented from being expressed; kept down
SYLLABICATION	Having to do with the parts of words

TERMINALLY	Irreversibly
TORMENT	Intense suffering
TRAJECTORY	Path a flying object takes
TRANQUILIZE	Administer a drug that will soothe or calm
TRANSLUCENCE	State of being semi-transparent

UNFURL	Spread out from a folded position
UNRULY	Hard to control
VERGE	A point or limit
VULGAR	Lacking charm, culture, or sophistication

View From Saturday Vocabulary

DIVERSITY	BRAWN	EXCESSIVE	SYLLABICATION	ACQUIRE
ORIGINATE	COMPLEMENTARY	RENDERING	NONCHALANTLY	INCUBATING
DICTATORIAL	UNRULY	FREE SPACE	ITINERANT	ACRONYMS
CONCLUDED	PRETEXT	PROTRUDING	APPOINT	KNOLL
REINFORCE	LECTERN	STRICT	UNFURL	ADORN

View From Saturday Vocabulary

ADVISED	ANIMATED	TERMINALLY	ATROCIOUSLY	VULGAR
TRANSLUCENCE	PRECEDED	FAVORABLE	SPONTANEOUS	JUBILANT
INVOLUNTARILY	INVENTORY	FREE SPACE	PRECEDENT	NATURALIZATION
PREOCCUPIED	SOPHISTICATED	INEVITABLE	MAIMED	REFRAINED
QUARTERING	AMBLED	DISENTANGLED	CONVERSION	CAPSULE

View From Saturday Vocabulary

ACQUIRE	ECOLOGY	DECORUM	CONVERSION	MEDIOCRE
VULGAR	PERPETUAL	REVISED	DIVERSITY	PARCELED
ADMONISH	TRAJECTORY	FREE SPACE	SUPPRESSED	ADORN
IRONIC	MALICE	ACRONYMS	TRANQUILIZE	BRAWN
SENTINELS	MECHANISM	SYLLABICATION	ITINERANT	TORMENT

View From Saturday Vocabulary

FRIEZE	QUARTERING	COIFFED	NEGLECT	RUCKUS
CONVERGED	ADVISED	GENUS	KNOLL	QUAINT
NONCHALANTLY	MAIMED	FREE SPACE	APPOINT	BENEVOLENTLY
SPONTANEOUS	ARCHIVE	PROTRUDING	VERGE	ACCURATE
EXCESSIVE	DISENTANGLED	FAVORABLE	DEFINITELY	MAMMOTH

View From Saturday Vocabulary

ITINERANT	PERPETUAL	UNFURL	ARCHIVE	ACQUIRE
RUCKUS	PRECEDED	INCUBATING	ADMONISH	DEFINITELY
PHALANX	FAVORABLE	FREE SPACE	NATURALIZATION	PRETEXT
MALICE	RENDERING	INEVITABLE	QUARTERING	GENUS
FRIEZE	ADVISED	SUPPRESSED	PREOCCUPIED	TRAJECTORY

View From Saturday Vocabulary

PRECISION	SYLLABICATION	SENTINELS	SOPHISTICATED	BRAWN
NANOSECOND	SPONTANEOUS	LECTERN	UNRULY	CARDINAL
JUBILANT	DISENTANGLED	FREE SPACE	BATED	APPOINT
TERMINALLY	CONVERSION	QUAINT	ACCURATE	VERGE
CONVERGED	MEDIOCRE	STRICT	MAMMOTH	HOVERED

View From Saturday Vocabulary

TORMENT	REFRAINED	ATROCIOUSLY	PRECEDENT	LECTERN
FRIEZE	PRECISION	GENUS	COIFFED	TRAJECTORY
FEEBLE	PRECEDED	FREE SPACE	PERPETUAL	DOMICILES
CAPSULE	CARAFE	DECORUM	TRANQUILIZE	PRETEXT
DIVERSITY	ADMONISH	UNRULY	DICTATORIAL	SENTINELS

View From Saturday Vocabulary

SPONTANEOUS	UNFURL	QUAINT	NANOSECOND	COMPLEMENTARY
DISENTANGLED	VULGAR	SUPPRESSED	ACRONYMS	ECOLOGY
BATED	NATURALIZATION	FREE SPACE	APPOINT	DEFACTO
PHALANX	MAIMED	PREOCCUPIED	BENEVOLENTLY	PARCELED
VERGE	INEVITABLE	CARDINAL	INVENTORY	ADVISED

View From Saturday Vocabulary

FEEBLE	FAVORABLE	DEFINITELY	SUPPRESSED	TRANSLUCENCE
DICTATORIAL	QUARTERING	CONVERSION	NANOSECOND	SOPHISTICATED
INEVITABLE	ARCHIVE	FREE SPACE	AMBLED	PROTRUDING
PERPETUAL	PRETEXT	REVISED	MAMMOTH	JUBILANT
RUCKUS	MEDIOCRE	ITINERANT	HOVERED	PREOCCUPIED

View From Saturday Vocabulary

UNFURL	SPONTANEOUS	CARDINAL	VULGAR	BRAWN
TERMINALLY	PRECISION	ATROCIOUSLY	DECORUM	TORMENT
BENEVOLENTLY	CONVERGED	FREE SPACE	ADMONISH	ACCURATE
ORIGINATE	REFRAINED	ANIMATED	STRICT	VERGE
SOVEREIGN	TRAJECTORY	COIFFED	NATURALIZATION	BATED

View From Saturday Vocabulary

TRANQUILIZE	PRETEXT	TRAJECTORY	BENEVOLENTLY	DEFACTO
NATURALIZATION	QUARTERING	PROTRUDING	SOVEREIGN	REFRAINED
UNRULY	ECOLOGY	FREE SPACE	BATED	ORIGINATE
DEFINITELY	INEVITABLE	SYLLABICATION	CONVERGED	CAPSULE
HOVERED	ACQUIRE	LECTERN	ANIMATED	JUBILANT

View From Saturday Vocabulary

FRIEZE	STRICT	CARDINAL	SUPPRESSED	RUCKUS
VULGAR	TRANSLUCENCE	APPOINT	PREOCCUPIED	COMPLEMENTARY
EXCESSIVE	ATROCIOUSLY	FREE SPACE	ADVISED	MECHANISM
REINFORCE	PRECEDED	PRECEDENT	VERGE	TERMINALLY
MEDIOCRE	DIVERSITY	PRECISION	DICTATORIAL	ADMONISH

View From Saturday Vocabulary

QUARTERING	SOVEREIGN	JUBILANT	REVISED	LECTERN
ECOLOGY	IRONIC	KNOLL	TERMINALLY	COIFFED
MAIMED	ACRONYMS	FREE SPACE	PREOCCUPIED	NONCHALANTLY
MAMMOTH	MEDIOCRE	UNFURL	FRIEZE	ADMONISH
PRECEDENT	MECHANISM	CONVERSION	TRAJECTORY	APPOINT

View From Saturday Vocabulary

ARCHIVE	SOPHISTICATED	ATROCIOUSLY	ITINERANT	NANOSECOND
DECORUM	GENUS	CARAFE	REINFORCE	BRAWN
CONCLUDED	PRECEDED	FREE SPACE	CARDINAL	VERGE
TRANQUILIZE	PROTRUDING	RUCKUS	CONVERGED	DEFINITELY
EXCESSIVE	INVOLUNTARILY	BATED	INCUBATING	DISENTANGLED

View From Saturday Vocabulary

INVENTORY	DECORUM	STRICT	BATED	BENEVOLENTLY
RENDERING	PERPETUAL	ADVISED	PRECEDED	REFRAINED
ECOLOGY	NANOSECOND	FREE SPACE	COIFFED	DEFACTO
TRAJECTORY	DOMICILES	SOPHISTICATED	HOVERED	ACCURATE
PRECISION	MALICE	JUBILANT	UNFURL	CONCLUDED

View From Saturday Vocabulary

PRETEXT	SOVEREIGN	INCUBATING	ARCHIVE	TRANQUILIZE
QUARTERING	PROTRUDING	NATURALIZATION	ACRONYMS	APPOINT
TERMINALLY	SUPPRESSED	FREE SPACE	UNRULY	ITINERANT
ORIGINATE	VERGE	IRONIC	MECHANISM	PRECEDENT
MEDIOCRE	SPONTANEOUS	REVISED	BRAWN	ADORN

View From Saturday Vocabulary

MALICE	IRONIC	SUPPRESSED	TORMENT	CONCLUDED
NANOSECOND	COMPLEMENTARY	EXCESSIVE	BATED	KNOLL
STRICT	TRAJECTORY	FREE SPACE	REINFORCE	SOPHISTICATED
DEFINITELY	INCUBATING	DIVERSITY	ITINERANT	CONVERGED
PRETEXT	MECHANISM	ACRONYMS	REFRAINED	ADORN

View From Saturday Vocabulary

SENTINELS	NEGLECT	ATROCIOUSLY	JUBILANT	VULGAR
SOVEREIGN	ADVISED	MAIMED	SPONTANEOUS	QUARTERING
DOMICILES	UNRULY	FREE SPACE	DICTATORIAL	HOVERED
GENUS	ACCURATE	BENEVOLENTLY	VERGE	PRECEDENT
ORIGINATE	QUAINT	CONVERSION	PRECEDED	ANIMATED

View From Saturday Vocabulary

NONCHALANTLY	FEEBLE	INVENTORY	ACRONYMS	ORIGINATE
TRANQUILIZE	PERPETUAL	NANOSECOND	PREOCCUPIED	JUBILANT
NEGLECT	TERMINALLY	FREE SPACE	AMBLED	ANIMATED
ADMONISH	FRIEZE	SPONTANEOUS	INCUBATING	QUAINT
APPOINT	BATED	COMPLEMENTARY	HOVERED	CARDINAL

View From Saturday Vocabulary

PHALANX	PRECEDENT	SYLLABICATION	ADORN	ITINERANT
TRANSLUCENCE	PARCELED	UNFURL	VERGE	REINFORCE
STRICT	REVISED	FREE SPACE	INVOLUNTARILY	CONVERGED
SENTINELS	DICTATORIAL	ATROCIOUSLY	CAPSULE	MAIMED
SOPHISTICATED	DEFACTO	TORMENT	GENUS	DEFINITELY

View From Saturday Vocabulary

BENEVOLENTLY	PREOCCUPIED	TRANSLUCENCE	CONCLUDED	SOPHISTICATED
NATURALIZATION	REINFORCE	PRECEDENT	SYLLABICATION	ARCHIVE
DICTATORIAL	CONVERGED	FREE SPACE	TORMENT	ANIMATED
STRICT	VERGE	COMPLEMENTARY	APPOINT	DISENTANGLED
KNOLL	PRETEXT	GENUS	COIFFED	INVENTORY

View From Saturday Vocabulary

INCUBATING	ECOLOGY	DEFINITELY	ADVISED	ADORN
ACQUIRE	DECORUM	LECTERN	IRONIC	CARAFE
RENDERING	MAIMED	FREE SPACE	SPONTANEOUS	QUAINT
NEGLECT	QUARTERING	EXCESSIVE	MAMMOTH	INEVITABLE
REVISED	AMBLED	CONVERSION	SOVEREIGN	VULGAR

View From Saturday Vocabulary

VERGE	CARDINAL	DOMICILES	ECOLOGY	TERMINALLY
GENUS	ADORN	INVOLUNTARILY	APPOINT	SPONTANEOUS
DICTATORIAL	NONCHALANTLY	FREE SPACE	ATROCIOUSLY	CONCLUDED
ORIGINATE	STRICT	MAIMED	ACCURATE	ADVISED
ARCHIVE	TRANSLUCENCE	ACRONYMS	TRAJECTORY	PRETEXT

View From Saturday Vocabulary

UNRULY	REFRAINED	DEFACTO	ANIMATED	UNFURL
PARCELED	SYLLABICATION	PRECEDENT	SOVEREIGN	BRAWN
CONVERSION	JUBILANT	FREE SPACE	NEGLECT	REINFORCE
MAMMOTH	COMPLEMENTARY	KNOLL	CONVERGED	INEVITABLE
DECORUM	TRANQUILIZE	MALICE	PROTRUDING	DEFINITELY

View From Saturday Vocabulary

SUPPRESSED	CARDINAL	NATURALIZATION	PERPETUAL	ADORN
EXCESSIVE	PARCELED	ECOLOGY	SYLLABICATION	NONCHALANTLY
HOVERED	DIVERSITY	FREE SPACE	MAMMOTH	ITINERANT
UNRULY	TRANQUILIZE	PRECEDENT	PRETEXT	ADMONISH
ADVISED	FEEBLE	NEGLECT	VULGAR	RENDERING

View From Saturday Vocabulary

KNOLL	CARAFE	LECTERN	APPOINT	PROTRUDING
ORIGINATE	MEDIOCRE	ATROCIOUSLY	REFRAINED	ACQUIRE
BATED	REVISED	FREE SPACE	DICTATORIAL	CONCLUDED
INVOLUNTARILY	FAVORABLE	DEFACTO	ANIMATED	RUCKUS
UNFURL	DOMICILES	SPONTANEOUS	IRONIC	PRECISION

View From Saturday Vocabulary

ITINERANT	TORMENT	ARCHIVE	JUBILANT	PERPETUAL
ECOLOGY	SUPPRESSED	ACRONYMS	COIFFED	DEFACTO
MALICE	INCUBATING	FREE SPACE	PRECISION	SYLLABICATION
NATURALIZATION	PARCELED	ANIMATED	DECORUM	DIVERSITY
TRANSLUCENCE	AMBLED	NONCHALANTLY	PRECEDED	NEGLECT

View From Saturday Vocabulary

ACQUIRE	PRECEDENT	ACCURATE	UNFURL	UNRULY
COMPLEMENTARY	QUARTERING	INVOLUNTARILY	SENTINELS	FRIEZE
SPONTANEOUS	MECHANISM	FREE SPACE	EXCESSIVE	SOVEREIGN
QUAINT	KNOLL	MAIMED	STRICT	LECTERN
IRONIC	GENUS	CARAFE	PREOCCUPIED	ADORN

View From Saturday Vocabulary

PROTRUDING	MEDIOCRE	DOMICILES	TRAJECTORY	FAVORABLE
VULGAR	FRIEZE	DECORUM	CARAFE	CONCLUDED
IRONIC	DISENTANGLED	FREE SPACE	JUBILANT	TRANQUILIZE
AMBLED	CARDINAL	CONVERSION	ADMONISH	RENDERING
RUCKUS	ACRONYMS	PRECEDED	PERPETUAL	PARCELED

View From Saturday Vocabulary

DIVERSITY	CAPSULE	SOVEREIGN	HOVERED	NEGLECT
PRETEXT	BATED	INVENTORY	UNRULY	ORIGINATE
QUARTERING	EXCESSIVE	FREE SPACE	MECHANISM	ACQUIRE
DEFINITELY	REINFORCE	DEFACTO	SENTINELS	TORMENT
STRICT	REVISED	ADORN	SUPPRESSED	PRECISION

View From Saturday Vocabulary

DEFINITELY	IRONIC	VERGE	DIVERSITY	CONVERSION
MAIMED	PARCELED	MAMMOTH	APPOINT	ECOLOGY
INEVITABLE	REVISED	FREE SPACE	MALICE	NEGLECT
DECORUM	TRANSLUCENCE	SOVEREIGN	ACQUIRE	CAPSULE
SPONTANEOUS	UNRULY	KNOLL	SYLLABICATION	ANIMATED

View From Saturday Vocabulary

QUARTERING	INVOLUNTARILY	VULGAR	PREOCCUPIED	DEFACTO
NATURALIZATION	PERPETUAL	SOPHISTICATED	TRANQUILIZE	ACRONYMS
AMBLED	CARAFE	FREE SPACE	FRIEZE	INCUBATING
TRAJECTORY	CONVERGED	ACCURATE	MEDIOCRE	PRECISION
SENTINELS	JUBILANT	SUPPRESSED	LECTERN	NONCHALANTLY

www.ingramcontent.com/pod-product-compliance
Lightning Source LLC
Chambersburg PA
CBHW081450070526
44586CB00019B/2293